CASE STUDIES IN
CULTURAL ANTHROPOLOGY

GENERAL EDITORS

George and Louise Spindler

STANFORD UNIVERSITY

CHINATOWN

*Economic Adaptation and
Ethnic Identity of the Chinese*

CHINATOWN

Economic Adaptation and
Ethnic Identity of the Chinese

By

BERNARD P. WONG

University of Wisconsin, Janesville

HOLT, RINEHART AND WINSTON

NEW YORK   CHICAGO   SAN FRANCISCO   PHILADELPHIA
MONTREAL   TORONTO   LONDON   SYDNEY   TOKYO
MEXICO CITY   RIO DE JANEIRO   MADRID

Library of Congress Cataloging in Publication Data

Wong, Bernard P.
  Chinatown, economic adaptation and ethnic identity
of the Chinese.

  (Case studies in cultural anthropology)
  Bibliography: p. 109
  1. Chinese Americans—New York (N.Y.)—Social con-
ditions. 2. Chinese Americans—New York (N.Y.)—Economic
conditions. 3. Chinese Americans—Social conditions.
4. Chinese Americans—Economic conditions. 5. Chinatown
(New York, N.Y.)—Social conditions. 6. Chinatown
(New York, N.Y.)—Economic conditions. 7. New York
(N.Y.)—Social conditions. 8. New York (N.Y.)—Economic
conditions. I. Title. II. Series.
F128.9.C5W65   305.8'951'07471   81-20015
ISBN 0-03-058906-1   AACR2

CBS COLLEGE PUBLISHING
Holt, Rinehart and Winston
The Dryden Press
Saunders College Publishing

To my wife Rosemarie

Foreword

ABOUT THE SERIES

These case studies in cultural anthropology are designed to bring to students, in beginning and intermediate courses in the social sciences, insights into the richness and complexity of human life as it is lived in different ways and in different places. They are written by men and women who have lived in the societies they write about and who are professionally trained as observers and interpreters of human behavior. The authors are also teachers, and in writing their books they have kept the students who will read them foremost in their minds. It is our belief that when an understanding of ways of life very different from one's own is gained, abstractions and generalizations about social structure, cultural values, subsistence techniques, and the other universal categories of human social behavior become meaningful.

ABOUT THE AUTHOR

Bernard P. Wong was born in China and has been educated in Hong Kong, China, the Philippines, and the United States. He holds a M.A. and a Ph.D. in anthropology from the University of Wisconsin–Madison. He has taught in Hong Kong and the United States. For the past seven years, he has been teaching anthropology at the University of Wisconsin, Janesville. He is also an Honorary Fellow of the Department of Anthropology, University of Wisconsin–Madison. Dr. Wong speaks several Chinese dialects, which has facilitated his research on the Chinese populations of the world. He has conducted field research in Manila, Singapore, Lima (Peru), New York City, and Wisconsin. Dr. Wong's areas of interest are ethnicity, economic anthropology, and urban and community studies. He is the author of *A Chinese American Community* (1979) and professional articles dealing with ethnic elites, social stratification, and assimilation published in *Urban Anthropology, Urban Life,* and *Comparative Studies in Society and History,* respectively.

Bernard Wong is currently Associate Professor of Anthropology, University of Wisconsin Center System.

ABOUT THE BOOK

The Chinese in the United States, like other nonAnglo-European minorities in this country, have experienced blatant prejudice and serious harassment. When they were no longer needed to build the western railroads in the 1870's, the Chinese were subject to flagrant attacks on their homes and business establishments (then just emerging) as well as on their persons—in at least one instance in the form of an outright massacre. They have been subject to persistent legal harassment in the form of exclusionary legislation, starting with the Exclusion Act of 1882 in California. In the 1930's, when the Chinese hand laundry business became too successful in New York, they were subject to state legislation requiring license fees and posting of bonds that forced many of the smaller establishments into bankruptcy. Legal harassment continued into the 1970's, including a law that prevented Chinese Americans from working in government positions. Although the most blatant forms of discrimination have recently eased, lingering and more subtle forms still persist.

This active prejudice and harassment stemming from mainstream American racism and fear of economic competition has resulted in the tightening of internal bonds within the minority group and the development of protective associations of one kind or another. The internal cohesiveness thus developed became the distinguishing characteristic of the Chinese American communities in cities like San Francisco and New York. These "Chinatowns" continue to serve the growing Chinese population in the United States in the various ways that Dr. Wong explains in this case study.

Federally funded social agencies have begun to compete with traditional associations in the Chinese enclave communities and the relationships between these associations and the social agencies have not been altogether peaceful. One may hypothesize that with the recent elimination of much federal support for social agencies and programs there will be a strengthening of the traditional associations.

This case study analyzes the structural adaptations that Chinese American communities in general, and the New York Chinatown in particular, have made to survive in American society. The analysis will be of interest to students of social life in the United States and particularly to those interested in minority groups and their struggles to find security and satisfaction. Although the Chinese adaptation has been different from that of the various European populations migrating to the United States after the Revolutionary War, and even from the Japanese and other Asiatic minorities, the Chinese exhibit much in common with other minorities in America.

To understand the adaptations of minorities in the United States is to understand our country since minority groups constitute our population. Even the so-called majority, or mainstream, in American society is made up of at least a dozen ethnic components, and its largest constituency—persons descended from the English, Scottish, Irish, and Welsh (themselves minorities in Great Britain)—is actually a minority of about 27 percent of our total population.

Dr. Wong's study therefore has wide applicability to the relationships among the ethnic components and between the ethnic components and the whole of our society. It is a study that provides solid information within a clear social–anthropological framework. It provides an analysis of Chinese adaptation to our society up to the present time, when many Chinese Americans live outside the Chinatowns and have entered into the lives of their residential communities at all levels of occupational and social prestige. Nevertheless, most Chinese Americans retain their identity and their relationships, in some form, with Chinese communities. Dr. Wong provides not only substantial data and a sound analytic framework but also enlivens his case study with biographical materials that help the student to understand something of life in the Chinese community from the inside.

GEORGE AND LOUISE SPINDLER
General Editors

Calistoga, California

Acknowledgments

I am indebted to many of the New York Chinatown residents who assisted me in my field work activities throughout the year. Andrew Chan, Kenny Kan, and Father Chang, among others, have been more than patient with my numerous visits and interviews. Chia-Ling Kuo also offered many good suggestions in the collection of data. My colleagues and students in the University of Wisconsin System gave me much encouragement in the writing of this work. Arnold Strickon, Robert Storch, Larry Young, and C. L. Kao all gave me valuable suggestions. Some data were collected during the summer of 1981 while I was attending the NEH (National Endowment for the Humanities) Faculty Seminar on China at Columbia University under the guidance of Dr. Myron Cohen. The initial field research, which was carried out in 1972 through 1973, was supported by a grant (GS–35279) from the National Science Foundation and a fellowship in ethnic studies from the Ford Foundation. Recent field work (1980–1981) was aided by a grant from the University of Wisconsin System Ethnic Studies Coordinating Committee. Finally, I am thankful to David Buchen for his photographic work, to Connie Olson for her typing of the manuscript, and to Elyce Misher for her helpful suggestions in editing the manuscript.

Contents

CASE STUDIES IN
CULTURAL ANTHROPOLOGY

GENERAL EDITORS
George and Louise Spindler
STANFORD UNIVERSITY

CHINATOWN

*Economic Adaptation and
Ethnic Identity of the Chinese*

1/From China to America

In major metropolitan areas such as New York City, Chicago, San Francisco, Los Angeles, and Boston, one can find a substantial number of the Chinese concentrated in the "Chinatowns." Why do Chinese Americans tend to inhabit urban areas and be involved in certain ethnic businesses? To understand the adaptive activities of Chinese Americans, one must have a basic knowledge of their migration history as well as their social, political, and economic environments.

A BRIEF HISTORY OF THE CHINESE IN AMERICA

When the Chinese first came to the New World is the subject of debate. According to Fang Zhongpu, a specialist in the history of navigation, Chinese Buddhists arrived in the Americas a thousand years before Columbus.[1] Other social scientists and historians believe that Chinese vessels probably visited the Pacific coastal regions of North America, including Mexico, more than a thousand years ago.[2] In any case, even if Chinese Buddhists did reach America in the fifth century, there was no follow-up migration of the Chinese to America until 1784, when the American trading vessels visited Canton. This was the first official Chinese–American contact, but the massive Chinese immigration movement did not begin until the 1950s. Why did the Chinese leave China to come to the United States?

In traditional China, before the nineteenth century, there was no great urge among the Chinese to emigrate as was the case among Western peoples who wanted to find new land and to separate themselves from the past and from their forebears (Hsu 1971:42). The Chinese had such strong feelings for the Middle Kingdom (as they called their country), that anyone who left it to live among foreigners was thought to be degrading himself (Morse 1918; Tien 1953; Hsu 1971). There was no protection for the Chinese who went abroad. Under the Manchu Dynasty (1644–1911), stiff penalties were given to persons who left the

[1] This date is cited in a magazine article published in China: "Did Chinese Buddhists Reach America 1,000 Years Before Columbus?" Fang Zhongpu, *China Reconstruct*, (August 1980: 65).

[2] For details consult the work of Joseph de Guignes, *Recherches sur les Navigations des Chinois du Cote de L'Amerique*. Paris: Académie des inscriptions, 1761.

1

country. Thus, any Chinese who went overseas did so at his own risk and could only rely on other Chinese immigrants for protection (Wong 1979). In fact, until 1894, any Chinese who left China were considered to be committing a capital offense (Morse 1918). In addition to legal difficulties and emotional stress, migrating Chinese had to endure the hardships of travel by junkboat or steamboat. Traveling conditions for Chinese contract laborers were so bad that many died before reaching their destinations; more than 200 laborers died on one such journey to Peru (Wong 1978, 1979; Tien 1953).

Any Chinese who wanted to go abroad had to consider these risks. Yet, despite these hardships, many individuals still decided to emigrate, due to the socioeconomic conditions in traditional China, and the opportunities in the United States.

Migration is an adaptive decision, a choice based on dissatisfaction with present life, calculation of available alternatives, and visions of a more desirable lot in the future. Nineteenth century China was beset with many political and economic problems. The Opium War (1839–1842) between China and Great Britain and the resultant Treaty of Nanking drained China's treasury. According to the Treaty, China had to forfeit Hong Kong and pay an indemnity of 21 million silver dollars to the British crown. During the latter part of the Manchu Dynasty, the Chinese Empire was further weakened by peasant riots and protests, one of which was the Taiping Rebellion of 1851–1864. As a result of this uprising millions of people were killed and the economy of China was ruined. Economic distress was particularly strong in the Kwangtung and Fukien provinces, which were very poor and overpopulated (Chen 1923; Wu 1958). Consequently, many Chinese were forced to seek their fortunes elsewhere.

In the nineteenth century the Chinese, especially those in the coastal regions of Fukien and Kwangtung, were aware of overseas opportunities. Fukienese usually migrated to the South Seas, and the Chinese from Sze Yap and Sam Yap districts, near Canton in the province of Kwangtung, came to the United States (R. Lee 1960; Wong 1979).

We may now understand the reasons for Chinese immigration, but we still do not know why they selected the United States as their destination. Some factors facilitating migration to the United States include: (1) previous connections, such as kinship, friendship, and even classmates; (2) civil or criminal offenses, local disturbances and family quarrels; (3) recruitment efforts of international labor brokers in Fukien and Kwangtung.

The first wave of the Chinese migration movement was triggered by the "gold rush" in California and by the American mining and railway companies which needed cheap labor (R. Lee 1960; Wong 1979). These economic opportunities in the United States drew the Chinese like a magnet. American and Chinese transportation agencies further facilitated the migration by providing passage and making travel arrangements for those whose relatives in America could make advance payment (R. Lee 1960). Many immigrants were paid in advance by their relatives and/or the employing companies in the United States. Thus, the Chinese migration to the United States in the nineteenth century was caused by the push of the Old Country and the pull of the New Country. Between 1850 and 1890 Chinese immigration continued to increase, and reached its peak in 1890.

Before 1880, most of the Chinese who migrated to the United States settled mainly in California and other Pacific coastal regions. Only after the various anti-Chinese campaigns in California (to be discussed later) and the subsequent passage of the Chinese Exclusion Law in 1882, did Chinese immigrants start to disperse into different parts of the country. The resulting Chinese influx into New York City can also be considered a collective adaptive device, which will be the subject of a later discussion.

FROM CALIFORNIA TO NEW YORK

The initial Chinese settlements in nineteenth century America clustered around the western link of the Transcontinental Railroad and the frontier states in the West. According to the census data of 1880, there were 105,464 Chinese in the U.S. Of this number, 87,828 (or 83 percent of the total Chinese in the U.S. at that time) settled in the Pacific coastal area, where they were principally engaged in mining, railroad construction, domestic service, and agriculture. The labor of these early immigrants built up the Western frontiers, especially the states of California, Washington, Oregon, Nevada, Utah, Idaho, Montana, Colorado, and Wyoming. Between 1850 and 1860 there were 61,397 Chinese laborers recruited to work for mining and railroad companies (R. Lee 1960; Barth 1964). In the 1850s Chinese mining camps began to spring up and dot the California countryside. By 1870, the Chinese became a major labor force, with 17,609 working as miners in California. Almost all of these miners were employed to exploit gold, silver, quick-silver, and coal deposits.

The Central Pacific Railway company at one time had 13,000 Chinese workers (80% of all the railroad laborers hired by the company) constructing the western part of the Transcontinental Railroad. In fact, both American mining and railway companies launched extensive advertising campaigns in and around Hong Kong and Canton to recruit Chinese laborers. One such advertisement, translated from the Chinese language, read:

> Americans, a very high people. They want the Chinaman to come and will make him very welcome. There you will have great pay, large houses, and food and clothing of the finest description. You can write to your friends and send them money at any time, and we will be responsible for the safe delivery, without mandarins or soldiers. All alike, big man no larger than little man. . . . Money is in great plenty and to spare in America. Such as wish to have wages and labor guaranteed can obtain the surety by application at this office.[3]

America welcomed the Chinese when it needed them to develop the West. Chinese workers not only built the western link of the Transcontinental Railroad ahead of schedule, but in so doing they also made many of the directors of the Central Pacific Company millionaires: Collis Huntington left an estate estimated between $50 and $90 million; Mark Hopkins, between $20 and $30 million; and

[3] This statement is from Russell H. Conway, *Why and How*, Why the Chinese Emigrate and the Means They Adopt for the Purpose of Reaching America. Boston: Lee and Shepard, 1871.

another director, Leland Stanford, founded Stanford University with $30 million.[4] However, as soon as the Transcontinental Railroad was completed, and the profits of the mining companies dwindled, Chinese laborers were no longer welcome. "The Chinese must go!" was the slogan echoed back and forth in California.

Much anti-Chinese legislation was enacted in the counties and state government of California, and there was blatant discrimination. One example of such discrimination was a San Francisco ordinance of 1870 which outlawed the Chinese pole method of peddling vegetables and carrying laundry. Traditionally, the Chinese carried heavy loads with a pole which is used as a fulcrum resting on the shoulders. The Sidewalk Ordinance of 1870, which prohibited people using poles to carry merchandise from walking on the sidewalk, was directed specifically against the Chinese since all non-Chinese used wagons or carts to peddle their goods. Consequently, Chinese peddlers in California who sold their vegetables by the pole method were driven out of business by this legislation. In San Francisco, various ordinances were enacted prohibiting the use of firecrackers and Chinese ceremonial gongs, which for the Chinese were important symbols of luck and implements for festivities. In 1875, an Anti-Queue Law was put into effect in San Francisco. Under Manchu law, Chinese men were required to comb their hair into long braids called queues. Cutting off their queues was a serious violation of Chinese law and a personal humiliation to the Chinese. After the passage of the Anti-Queue Law, gangs of roughnecks began to attack Chinese people with long hair; their braids or "pigtails" were chopped off and worn as belts and caps by the hoodlums.

There were numerous laws prohibiting the Chinese from working in the government and the fishing business, the education of Chinese children in the public schools, and the use of Chinese as witnesses against Whites in court. In addition to the laws of county and state, the Congress, in 1882, passed the "Chinese Exclusion Law," which prohibited Chinese laborers from entering the country.

Many writers and historians believed that the cause of the anti-Chinese feelings in the Western states was principally due to economic competition, which did indeed precipitate the anti-Chinese movement and the passage of the Exclusion Law. White laborers often considered the Chinese as rivals for employment, because the Chinese worked hard and were willing to accept low wages. The anti-Chinese sentiment became so strong that many white employers in California were afraid to hire Chinese laborers. Resentment sometimes led to persecution and even massacre in some places. In 1880, in the Cherry Creek Diggings in Denver, bands of white ruffians toured the Chinese section, beating the inhabitants and looting their homes and places of business. The worst massacre of Chinese occurred in Rock Springs, Wyoming, on September 2, 1885, where more than 28 Chinese were murdered and many others were critically wounded. Anti-Chinese agitation continued to be particularly intense in California, even after the passage of the "Chinese Exclusion Law." Riots took place in the small towns and cities, such as Fresno, Sacramento, Los Angeles, San Jose, Pasadena, Napa, Chico, Vallejo, Redding, Santa Cruz, Locke, etc. It is no wonder that the Chinese had to plan new

[4] For more details, consult Wei Min She, *Chinese Working People in America*. San Francisco: United Front Press, 1974.

adaptive strategies, such as geographical relocation from California and other hostile states, to the eastern and central states.

For those who chose to go east, New York City was a favorite destination (see Figure 1).

A SHORT HISTORY OF NEW YORK'S CHINATOWN

The earliest Chinese resident of New York is thought to be Lee Ah-bow,[5] who came to New York City from San Francisco in 1850 via the S.S. *Valencia*. He was reported to be a cook, who later entered the tea business and died at the age of 90 in the state hospital for the criminally insane.

Figure 1   Chinatown Today.

[5] The question of who was the first Chinese immigrant in New York City is debatable. For more information consult Louis Beck, *New York's Chinatown*, New York: Bohemia Publishing Co., 1898; Calvin Lee, *Chinatown, U.S.A.* Garden City, N.Y.: Doubleday, 1965.

According to Louis Beck,[6] the second Chinese resident to settle in New York's Chinatown was Loy Hoy Sing, who settled on Cherry Street in 1862. The earliest Chinese resident of Mott Street is thought to be Ah Ken, who lived there in 1858. Large numbers of Chinese, however, did not come to New York City until after California's anti-Chinese campaign of the 1880s. In 1890, the Chinese population of New York had grown to 2,559.

Early Chinatown consisted of three streets: Mott, Park, and Doyer, where the majority of the early Chinese immigrants settled (see Figure 2) (Beck, 1898; Berger, 1957; Kung, 1962). This core area slowly increased in size, until New York's Chinatown covered the entire space bounded by Mott, Pell, and Doyer Streets, Chatham Square, and, by 1898, included Bayard and Baxter Streets (see Figure 2).

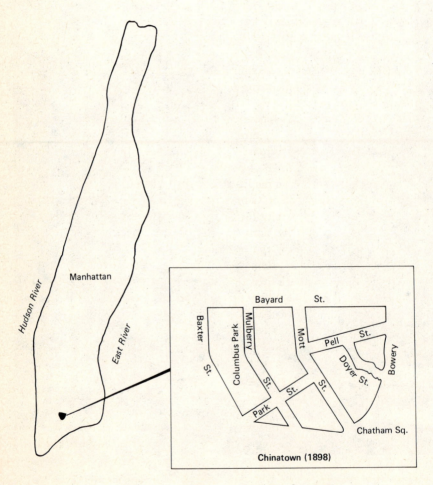

Figure 2   Chinatown, New York (1898).

---

[6] Wei Min She, *Chinese Working People in America.*

The development of New York's Chinatown underwent some major phases relating to the social, political, and economic climates of the larger society and the mother country of the Chinese immigrants.

Initial Development

1870 to 1884   The nucleus of the community was already formed during this period. It began with a population of 120 in 1870, which grew to about 500 in 1873. This small community consisted largely of Chinese males who worked as servants, cooks, stewards in hotels, clubhouses, or steamboats, or as vendors of Chinese candy (*New York Times*, July 26, 1873).

1884 to 1920   During this period, the Chinese population in New York City grew to 5,042 in 1920. It is interesting that while the number of Chinese in New York City increased during these years, the number of Chinese in the United States as a whole actually decreased. As mentioned earlier, massive unemployment created hotbeds for unrest and economic competition as well as conflicts between the Chinese and the White laborers. Unemployed Chinese laborers flooded the frontier towns, especially those of California, which created a "visibility" problem. Racist sentiments and economic competition thus compelled the Chinese to find new homes.

By 1920, 50 percent of the Chinese population living in the United States had dispersed into the Atlantic and Central states. New York City was attractive to Chinese immigrants for many reasons: (1) it was a vast city with many different races, a place where a small group of newly arrived immigrants would not "stand out"; (2) since it was located on the East coast, New York City was less influenced by the anti-Chinese sentiment of California (Wu 1958); (3) New York City offered more economic opportunity for Chinese who did not want to be laborers; and (4) a major city like New York could supply adequate clientele to Chinese businesses, such as hand laundry and restaurants.

Not that the Chinese came from a nation of laundrymen or restauranteurs! They selected these new careers after 1884, in an effort to avoid competition with White laborers in the labor market. The unpleasant memory of the consequences of competing with Whites in the labor market in California was still fresh. Hand laundry was considered women's work and Chinese restaurants required Chinese ethnic skill. As such, there could be no competition with White people and the Chinese people could now be self-employed or small businessmen. Chinese restaurants and laundries remain the most important businesses in New York's Chinatown.

1921 to 1948   Before 1945, there were very few women and children in Chinatown. Most of the population were male sojourners who had no intention of making permanent homes in the United States. The practice among these sojourners was to return to China periodically to get married and sire children. After a brief visit to China, they returned to the U.S. to continue their business, in the hope of accumulating enough wealth through hard work to retire to China and live a life of leisure. Those American-born Chinese who were U.S. citizens and could not find Chinese mates also returned to China to get married. Their children were given the right of derivative citizenship and were permitted to enter the U.S. This led to abuses. Since immigration from China to the U.S. was rendered extremely difficult, a slot system of "paper son" was devised by the Chinese in America. Some of the American-born Chinese falsely reported the birth of sons in China and thus created eligibility slots for future immigrants. Prospective immigrants would then buy these slots or papers to migrate to the U.S. under the pretext of joining their fathers (more appropriately called "paper fathers"). Illegal practices aside, some Chinese truly had their families and children in China, and they were not permitted to join their fathers unless the latter were U.S. citizens. The fact that they were legal residents of the U.S. was not sufficient to sponsor their families. Families were thus separated for years until the father returned to China for a visit and family life was jeopardized. This lack of family life and Chinese women also gave rise to the prosperity of prostitution, which was almost the sole business of the Tongs in the exclusion era. Another reason for the small number of Chinese women in the pre-1945 era was the U.S. immigration policy (which resulted from the Immigration Act of 1924), which restricted the admission of Chinese women because they were ineligible for citizenship (Kung 1962:97; Lee 1960:23). Because of this Act, many families were separated for as long as two decades. After World War II, however, because a large number of men in the American Armed forces, who were stationed overseas, married Nationals of foreign countries, Congress passed the War Bride Act of December 28, 1945, and the GI Fiancees' Act of June 29, 1946. Consequently, the wives and children of Chinese GIs or ex-servicemen of Chinese descent used this opportunity to emigrate to this country. Older informants remember this period as the first time they saw young Chinese women and children living in the community.

Communist Takeover in China (1949–1964)   Because of political changes in China, some Chinese students, professionals, trainees, visitors, and government officials were "stranded" in the United States. The establishment of the People's Republic also caused some Chinese to leave China. In 1953, the U.S. government passed the Refugee Relief Act and many of these Chinese refugees were admitted to this country. Due to the immigration of the Chinese refugees to the community, Chinese professionals and Mandarin-speaking and Shanghainese-speaking Chinese were together in one place for the first time.

The Chinese community in the pre-1965 era can be described as relatively homogeneous, highly segregated, and self-governed. In terms of origin, more than 99 percent of the Chinese came from the Kwangtung Province (mostly from Toysan), and the remainder came from Fukien and other parts of China. Since most of the Chinese in New York City were from Toysan, it was natural that Toysanese became the *lingua franca* of this community,[7] even though the Toysan dialect is only a variation of the standard Cantonese dialect spoken in the Kwangtung Province. In fact, Cantonese and Toysanese are so different that they are unintelligible to each other. Thus, in order to be accepted into the community in those days, a Cantonese had to learn the Toysan dialect. One informant related an anecdote to me about a Mandarin-speaking Chinese man who ordered his dinner

[7] Toysan is a county in the Kwangtung Province.

in a Toysanese restaurant, and was reprimanded with the comment, "What a shame, a Chinese who cannot even speak the Chinese language!"

The majority of the Chinese during this period were engaged in the operation of small laundries and restaurants, and it was the Toysanese who dominated these two trades. Very few Chinese had college educations, since they originally intended to work as laborers. This partially explains why so few Chinese could speak English well. Since there was no great demand for English-speaking people in these occupations, the Chinese had no incentive to improve their language skills once they were settled in their businesses.

Chinatown before 1965 was predominantly adult male. No wonder there were no juvenile delinquents in those days! On the other hand, many considered the absence of family life and children to be the main reason that the Chinese in New York City did not assimilate during this period. Other factors such as social organizations, limited economic opportunity, education, and attitudes of the larger society toward the Chinese and vice-versa also played a role in this situation.

1965–Present: A New Era   In many respects New York City's Chinatown has changed drastically since 1965. The boundaries of Chinatown have been enlarged, and demographic characteristics, such as occupation, population, locality of origin, community organization, and attitudes toward the larger society, have all been altered. One of the most important reasons for these changes is the Immigration Law of 1965.

As has been mentioned, in past years the United States has implemented several immigration policies affecting the Chinese. However, the 1965 Immigration Law abolished the "national origin" quotas and established a system of preferences, whereby immediate relatives, skilled and unskilled workers, refugees, scientists, and technical personnel were listed under different categories of preferences. And for the first time, Chinese immigrants were treated equally with other nationalities by the administration, thus ending some 83 years of immigration laws biased against the Chinese. Many Chinese once again flocked to this country, and consequently, the Chinese population of New York City swelled to a record high of 69,000 in 1970 (U.S. Census of Population, 1970).

According to estimates by my informants, 80,000 more Chinese have come to New York City since 1965. This puts the Chinese population in New York City in 1980 at approximately 150,000. Of this number, 75,000 are said to reside in the Chinatown area. Thus, only about 50 percent of the Chinese in New York City stay in the Chinatown area. Other areas of Chinese concentration are in the vicinities of Columbia University, Flatbush, Jackson Heights, and the Elmhurst section of Queens.

The increase of the Chinese population in Chinatown has a direct effect on the boundaries of Chinatown (see Figure 3). Today's Chinese population on the Lower East Side has expanded north to 14th Street, south to the piers, east to Allen Street, and west to Broadway. The commercial areas of Chinatown have branched out from Mott, Pell, Bayard, and Doyer to include Mulberry, Canal, Bowery, East Broadway, Catherine, Hester, Elizabeth, and Grand. Thus, both the residential and commercial areas of Chinatown have expanded, and other ethnic territories have been penetrated.

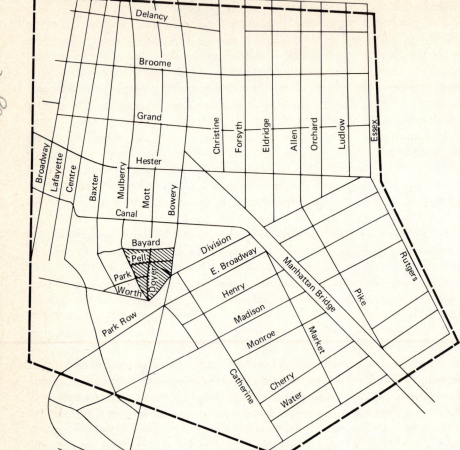

Figure 3   Chinatown, New York (1981).

The 1965 Immigration Law and the subsequent Chinese migration to New York City has not only changed the geographical boundaries and the population size, but also the social and economic characteristics of the people of Chinatown. Chinatown is now occupied by Chinese who intend to stay in the United States permanently. Although people from Kwangtung still make up more than half the population, there are people from North China, Shanghai, Hong Kong, Fukien, Taiwan, and even Cuba. The *lingua franca* is no longer Toysanese but the standard Cantonese spoken in the cities of Hong Kong, Macao, and Canton. Speakers of other dialects, such as Mandarin, Fukienese, Shanghainese, and Hakka have to learn the Cantonese dialect of Chinatown in order to communicate with the natives.

The female population has grown gradually since 1945; but only after 1965 did the male/female ratio narrow significantly. In 1970 the sex ratio nearly became equal: 37,504 males to 31,820 females. Today, approximately 10,000 Chinese women constitute a solid work force for the 300 Chinese garment factories in the Chinatown area.

Whereas the majority of the Chinese population from 1870 to 1965 had little or no education, a larger portion of Chinatown's population had received better educations after 1965. By 1969 the Chinese population had a relatively large number of college graduates. According to the *Chinatown Study Group Report* (1969), 35 percent of the 20- to 29-year-olds had a college and/or postgraduate education. This figure was very close to the national average for the U.S. population of the same age group living in metropolitan areas: 33.8 percent with college and postgraduate work. According to a survey of the same study group mentioned above, out of a sample of 1,361 Chinese, 743 have 12 years education. This amounts to 54.7 percent of the sample. Not only have people in Chinatown been more educated since 1965, but also more educated people have been migrating to the United States during this period.

The increase in and diversity of the population was also responsible for the multiplication and specialization of Chinese firms. For instance, Chinese restaurants were established to serve customers from different parts of China, making non-Cantonese cuisine available, such as Szechuan, Hunan, Peking, and Shanghai. Due to the availability of large numbers of seamstresses, the Chinese garment industry is a major source of income for the Chinese. New modes of organization and management reflect adaptation to modern technology and management techniques. Partnerships and chain stores have been added to traditional family firms. Besides the one-man or family laundry, washing plants, pressing plants, folding and marketing plants, and self-service laundromats have become popular. More Chinese are currently employed in non-Chinese establishments as professionals. All things considered, Chinatown is more outwardly oriented than in the past.

2/Social structure of Chinatown

CHINATOWNS IN GENERAL

The organization of most of America's Chinatowns follows the same principles. Not only does a Chinatown have its "unofficial city hall" and its "unofficial mayor,"[1] but many of its organizations, known as "associations," or *Wui Kung* (*Hui Kuan* in Mandarin), are in fact interrelated and form a national organizational network (see Figure 4). Within each Chinatown, there are family name, hometown, occupational, political, regional and linguistic associations which constitute the formal social structure. These associations are organized according to traditional principles of social organization (to be discussed later in the chapter) in the home communities of the early Chinese immigrants.

The traditional associations had more control over the Chinese residents in the past than they do in the present. Since 1965, in response to the needs of the new immigrants, other organizations have been established, and these were patterned after the modern voluntary associations common in many urban centers around the world[2] as well as the service organizations popular in America.[3]

SOCIAL STRUCTURE OF NEW YORK'S CHINATOWN

Chinatown's social structure today is a result of historical processes, and an end-product of concommitant interactions between Chinese and American society. New York City's Chinatown, like Chinatowns elsewhere in the U.S., have many features in common. The peculiar compositions of the social structures of America's

---

[1] They are unofficial because, strictly speaking, Chinatowns are not considered cities. The "unofficial city hall" refers to groups like the Chinese Consolidated Benevolent Association and the like which coordinate the affairs of the traditional Chinese immigrants. The head of the Chinese Consolidated Benevolent Association is labeled as the "unofficial mayor." These terms are not used by members of the community but are labels used by the general American public.

[2] Examples of these are the Lions, the Rotary Club, the Alumni Club, . . . etc.

[3] Service organizations include the social service agencies and brokerage institutions like employment agencies, travel agencies, and various forms of referral services.

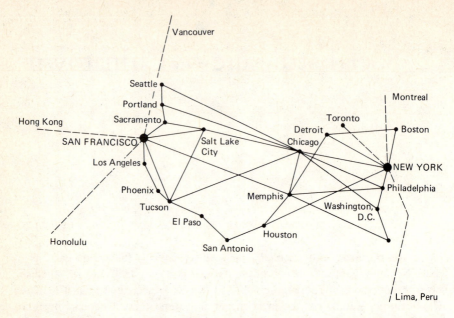

Figure 4   Network of Chinese Associations in the United States. The two major associational centers are San Francisco and New York.

Chinatowns reflect also the complexity of the economic system, contemporary politics, and urban life in America. These traditional organizations, though not as important as in the past, still persist in Chinatown and play a role in its social and economic life. In New York City's Chinatown, the traditional organizations constitute one of the three facets of the community social structure. The other two facets consist of the new associations and the social service agencies (see Figure 5).

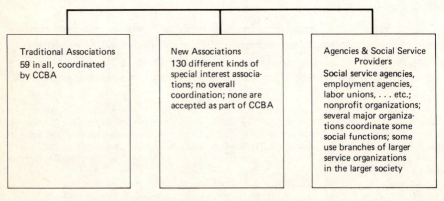

Figure 5   Social structure of Chinatown, New York.

THE TRADITIONAL ASSOCIATIONS

It is common among overseas Chinese to interact with people who share the same dialect, locality of origin, and family name. The Chinese in New York City are no exception. Hence the organizational structure of the traditional associations was derived from principles of the mother country, such as territoriality, kinship, linguistic (or dialectal) similarities, friendship, trade, and secret societies. Some of the organizations were shaped by political events, traditional structural features and other historical antecedents in nineteenth century China. In short, the organizational principles of the traditional associations were deeply rooted in the home communities, especially in the rural areas of Kwangtung. The American versions of these are not exact duplicates of the traditional Chinese organization; rather, they were modified to suit the American situation.

Chinatown's community structure is a hierarchy with the Chinese Consolidated Benevolent Association (CCBA) at the top as an overall organization in most of the major Chinatowns in America (see Figure 6). In New York City's Chinatown, this is no exception. The CCBA in New York, which coordinates the 59 trade, recreational, tong, regional, dialect, political, family name associations, is still the highest authority in Chinatown's traditional social structure. The lowest level organization, which was formerly coordinated by the CCBA, is known locally as *fong*, and is the village association that organizes people in terms of locality of origin and kinship relations.

The CCBA

Although the American name has changed from time to time depending upon the administration, there has only been one overall Chinese community organization, and the Chinese name remains, "Jung Wa Gung So" (The Chinese Public

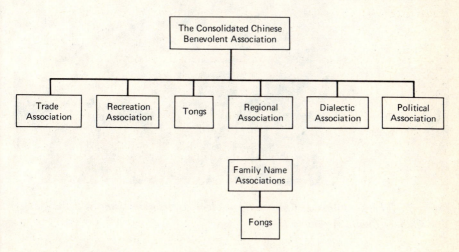

Figure 6   Chinatown's Traditional Associations.

Assembly Hall). The larger social units above the fongs were and still are the various clan or family name associations, which are known locally as *Gung So* (Public Assembly) or *Jung Chan Wui*[4] (Common Descent Relatives Association). "Jung Wa Gung So" is *not* a consulate or embassy. It was formed as an adaptation to a situation where necessary assistance could not be obtained from either the home country or the host country. The first "Jung Wa Gung So" (*Chung Hua Kung So* in Mandarin) was the Chinese Six Companies, established in 1869 (Hoy 1942:19–23) in San Francisco; it was composed of Chinese immigrants from the six major districts in Kwangtung, China: Ning Young, Hop Wo, Kong Chow, Yung Wood, Sam Yup, and Yan Wu. The "Jung Wa Gung So" in New York began in 1884 (Kuo 1977; Wong 1979), after many family name and regional associations failed to solve the community's problems. Many disputes such as those between members of two associations, or two tongs, could not be settled without a third party. The Consolidated Chinese Benevolent Association came into being in response to this special need (see Figure 7). According to its by-laws, the Association registered with the Peking Imperial Government in 1884 under the title of *Jung Wa Gung So* and was officially incorporated in 1890 under the Societies Act of New York State. The official name of Jung Wa Gung So at that time was the Chinese Charitable and Benevolent Association.

Figure 7   The Consolidated Chinese Benevolent Association (Jung Wa Gung So— The Chinese Public Assembly Hall).

[4] In Mandarin, it is pronounced as *Chung Chin Hui*.

The charitable functions of the *Jung Wa Gung So* were to offer educational and recreational services to its members. Since the old days, *Jung Wa Gung So* has run a Chinese school. Therefore, one can call it an agent of cultural stability and a conservative force on Chinese culture in the United States. In the past, the *Jung Wa Gung So* spoke for the Chinese community quite frequently. Today, there are other agencies and competing organizations that want to serve as a bridge between the community and the larger society. The president of CCBA was and still is the patron for the community, and has made friends and connections through his attendance at meetings and his performance of other functions on behalf of the community. In New York City, the president of the CCBA is referred to by outsiders as the "unofficial mayor of Chinatown."

The Consolidated Chinese Benevolent Association, the highest community organization, was supposed to insure the well-being of the Chinese, particularly their businesses. Up until 50 years ago, the CCBA had specific regulations about business locations for Chinese laundries and restaurants and performed mediation services to solve the disputes arising from these businesses. Although it no longer provides many of these functions, the CCBA remains the highest authority of the community.

The CCBA, like other traditional associations in New York's Chinatown, was established before 1965 to serve the needs of the adult male Chinese who were the main constituents of the community. It is not adequately prepared to tackle the contemporary social problems of the new immigrants, such as housing, medicare, employment, and youth problems. For this reason, the CCBA has been under attack from radical students and community workers for being too slow to adapt and meet the needs of the new immigrants. Also, many new, competing associations and agencies are being established to serve the needs of the new immigrants.

Kinship as Principle of Organization

In the home communities of the Chinese Americans, kinship relations were used to organize social and economic life. Many villages consisted of single lineages. Thus, an entire village may bear the same surname and its members may be related to each other by blood traceable to a common ancestor. This kind of single lineage village was not uncommon in the rural areas of Kwangtung (Freedman 1958). There were also villages which consisted of several lineages and thus of several kinship groups with several surnames.

Lineage in the home communities of the Chinese Americans is patrilineal and exogamous. The group shares a common ancestor associated with a locality. The males are members of the lineage; the women became members of their husband's lineage after they marry. In traditional China membership in the lineages is ascriptive. Although the principle of lineage is used in the family name associations of Chinese Americans, members are reunited solely on the basis of common surname; members may or may not share common blood or locality ties. For instance, Chinese Americans may unite the surnames Huang and Wang in one family name association, even though the Wang and Huang historically have many different lineages. In fact the Huang and Wang were not related at all, but they are joined together because the Cantonese pronunciation of the two names is the same: Wong.

The largest family name associations in New York City are those of Lee, Chan, Eng, and Wong. Within the family name associations are fongs which group people according to both common surname and common village of origin. Thus the *fongs* resemble more closely the lineage organizations of traditional China.

Anthropologically speaking, it is more appropriate to address the family name association as a clanship organization, because its members are only *assumed* to have descended from a common ancestor. There is no demonstrable consanguineal relationship among members. The use of lineage and clanship relationships to organize and group people in Chinese communities overseas fulfilled a need for the early immigrants (usually adult males who were married but had left their wives in China). These immigrants, who lacked family life and were unfamiliar with local customs and languages could call on one another for help, or generate family feelings or the atmosphere of brotherhood. The Chinese in the early days of New York's Chinatown depended entirely on these *fongs* and clan associations to solve the problems they encountered.

In rural China, every man belonged to a lineage. However, in the Chinese American communities, some of the Chinese had no chance to join any family name association. Thus for instance, in New York City's Chinatown, out of the 150 common surnames, not more than 60 of them were represented in the 29 family name associations. The fongs and family name associations perform functions similar to those in the homeland:

1. Social functions: members gather together to recreate and celebrate Chinese holidays
2. Rituals: family name associations worship their ancestors and pay homage to members who died
3. Dispute settlement
4. Welfare: some family name associations have credit clubs, translation services, temporary lodging facilities for the unemployed and the aged.

Although many of the members are not related to each other consanguineously, kinship ideology is deliberately embraced. Kinship terms like *Hing* (older brother), *Dai* (younger brother), *Shuk* (younger uncle), and *Bak* (older uncle) are commonly used.

In order to have a large membership, smaller surname groups united with each other according to traditional family alliances—both fictive and real—traditional friendship, sworn brotherhood, neighboring home districts in China, or similarity of a radical in the writing of surnames. These smaller surname groups form the multifamily name associations. One of these is the "Four Brothers" (see Figures 8 and 9) association, which was organized by the Liu, Kwan, Chang, and Chao families because their forebears swore brotherhood by the "Peace Garden Oath" 2000 years ago for the purpose of saving the Han Dynasty. Another multifamily name association is the G.H. Oak Tin Association, which is composed of the Chan,

Figure 8   The "Four Brothers" Association.

Figure 9   The Ancestor Altar in a Family Association.

Hu, and Yuan families who were traditionally united by friendship. The most interesting of all is the Chiu Lung Association which united the Tan, Tam, Hsu, and Hsieh families because all of them possess a common radical in their names.

The organizational principles of the fongs and family name associations had their origins in China but are modified to suit the needs of the Chinese Americans.

Regional and Linguistic Associations

Next to family and kinship, common geographical origin provides a most important basis for voluntary associations in traditional China. There are different levels of regionalism: provincial, city level, county level, township, village, sub-village, (e.g., territory within a village). Sometimes, a larger regional area such as northern China or southern China was also used.

Regional associations in New York's Chinatown roughly parallel their counterparts in China. The Ning Young Association was and still is the largest regional association; it has a large membership and financial resources, and is composed of members from the Toysan district of China. Another tremendous organization in

New York City's Chinatown is *Lun Sing*, whose members come from all other regions.

Various social scientists have attributed different causes for the development of regional associations. The structural functionalists stress the "conservative function" of regional associations in culture change: to build alignment according to traditional social order. The neo-Marxists argue that regional associations are a product of unequal development. Data obtained from the Chinese American communities, however, indicate that regional associations developed basically to provide mutual protection and to bridge the gap of kinship for early immigrants who were without family and family life. Regional associations in New York's Chinatown are also responsible for the election of the president of the overall community organization. In New York, the president of the CCBA is elected from the *Ning Young* and *Lun Sing* associations, on a rotating basis. Regional associations, like family name associations, are also mutual aid societies.

Most of the regional associations in New York City's Chinatown have their territorial and linguistic bases in China Thus the Ning Young association is composed of members from the Toysan district who speak the Toysan dialect. The *Wa Pak* (or Hua Pei in Mandarin) Association recruits members from northern China who speak the Mandarin dialect. An association which is organized solely in terms of dialect is the Hakka Association, whose members come from all over China, but all speak some forms of Hakka. Thus, in Chinatown, every Chinese is eligible to join at least one of the traditional associations: fongs, family name, regional, or linguistic associations.

These associations often act as traditional "credit clubs." For instance, the Lee family Association has its own credit union; however, banks and other financial institutions are the main sources of financing. Other important activities of these associations include the annual election of officials and the Spring and Autumn Sacrifice. To get elected, candidates donate thousands of dollars for community activities. The names of donors are then publicized by the local Chinese newspapers which circulate to Chinese communities throughout the United States. Thus those who run for office enjoy great publicity. The elected leaders of the associations still enjoy prestige in the business community, and such prestige can be converted into entrepreneurial pursuit. Once a person is a *kiu ling* (leader of the overseas Chinese),[5] he is invited to participate in partnerships and other gainful pursuits.

During the spring and autumn memorial services, leaders organize trips to the cemetery where former members have been buried. Then the participants return to the association hall for a collective ritual ceremony, bowing in front of the portraits of the ancestral leaders or the ancestral tablets of the Association, and a banquet is served. These associations remain a center for the recreation of the elderly and especially for the nostalgic Chinese who have strong emotional ties with the homeland and with Chinese culture. They can play Chinese games, speak in their own dialect, and celebrate Chinese festivals.

Various public social agencies have taken many welfare responsibilities from the

---

[5] *Kiu Ling* is pronounced as *Chiao Lin* in Mandarin. It means leaders of the overseas Chinese.

traditional family, regional, and dialectic associations. For instance, there are churches and social agencies serving the senior citizens.

Occupational and Trade Associations

Although merchant associations and occupational associations existed in pre-modern China, they did not become important in the Chinese American communities until 1930. In New York, the *Chinese Hand Laundry Alliance* was established in 1933; the *Chinese-American Restaurant Association* was also established in 1933; the *Chinese Seamen Association* was founded in 1943; and the *Chamber of Commerce* in 1930. These associations functioned to safeguard ethnic businesses. Many of them were formed in response to pressure from the larger society. For instance, in the 1930s there were systematic attacks against the Chinese laundry firms in New York City. Placards, cartoons, etc., depicted Chinese laundrymen at work spitting on white shirts. At this time regulations in New York State required each hand laundry to pay $25 for licensing and to post a $1,000 bond. This regulation forced many laundries to go bankrupt. These two events made the Chinese feel the importance of solidarity and the necessity of organizing themselves for mutual protection (Wong 1974:104). In May of 1933, the Chinese Hand Laundry Alliance was born. The leaders of the Alliance immediately explained the financial difficulties of the Chinese to the Public Welfare Committee of the Aldermanic Board of New York. As a result, the license fees for the laundry men were reduced to $10, and the security bond was reduced to $100. To avoid unnecessary and unhealthy competition, the Chinese Hand Laundry Association divided New York City into 30 laundry districts. Each district consisted of 10 laundries. Of the 300 delegates from the 30 districts, 104 were chosen to serve on the executive committee (Wong 1974). Similarly, other measures were taken in other trade associations to protect the Chinese tradesmen.

Today, trade associations have become even more important than in previous decades. The American-Chinese Restaurant Association and the Chinese Chamber of Commerce both have increased membership. They often negotiate with the larger society on matters of concern to Chinese businessmen. As information centers, they channel information and regulations on taxes, sanitation, wages, and licenses. These business or trade associations also advise their members about technical and legal details and to protect the interests of the Chinese businessmen.

Better educational background among Chinese businessmen is perhaps responsible for the membership increase in other businessmen's organizations, such as the Chinese-American Elks Club, Dragon Lodge, Lions Club of Chinatown, and the Chinese Chamber of Commerce. The most important of these is the Chinese Chamber of Commerce, which has recruited many influential Chinese businessmen. The Chinese Chamber of Commerce has acted both as patron and broker for the Chinese in recent years. Leaders of the Chamber are rich Chinese entrepreneurs who have donated generously to cultural activities in the community. These leaders have also sponsored community projects, such as the construction of the 29-story Confucius Plaza Cooperative, the installation of pagoda telephone booths and police call boxes with instructions in Chinese.

Leaders of the Chamber of Commerce are instrumental in transmitting valuable information to the community concerning economic opportunities, availability of government subsidies, and business regulations. For instance, the Chinese Chamber of Commerce urged the community and Chinese bussinessmen to take advantage of the "Mitchell-Lama Act," "The Housing Act of 1949," and the "Small Business Investment Act" to procure governmental aid to build better housing, parking facilities, and to make general improvements.

Chinese Chamber of Commerce leaders are brokers and patrons for the community. Their payoff is "prestige," which can be used in their own entrepreneurial activities. Many less prosperous Chinese businessmen look up to these leaders (their wealth, power, and possession of valuable information), and try to form contracts with them.

Tongs

The Tongs (or Tang in Mandarin) in American Chinatowns bear some resemblance to the secret societies in traditional China. They were both cloaked with the oath of secrecy, and were *initially* established to fight against the Manchu dynasty in Imperial China. They were also in the service (either fully or partially) of the Republican cause championed by Dr. Sun Yat-sen. One of the most active secret societies in the home communities of the early Chinese immigrants was "The Triad or Hung League." Many of the members of the Triad emigrated to the ports, mines, and plantations of the European colonies; some came to America.[6]

The North American branch of the Triad was first established in 1858 in British Canada.[7] By 1863, a branch was also formed in San Francisco.[8] Thereafter, every major Chinatown in the U.S. had a branch. The Triad (also known as Chee Kung Tong) in the U.S. was originally a political organization against Imperial China, but it was also involved in organized crimes: racketeering, white slave traffic, gambling, and prostitution. Some of its dissident members subsequently organized rival tongs in America: On Leong Tong; Hip Sing Tong; Ying On Tong; Bing Kung Tong; and Sui Ying Tong. In New York the On Leong Tong and the Hip Sing Tong were the most powerful. During the Tong Wars of the 1920s, the Tongs were frequently involved in murderous feuds. Because of the ill reputation they earned from their illegal businesses and their notorious tong wars, some of them "reformed" and changed their tongs into merchant associations. Some never recovered at all.

Scholars of Chinese Americans also see the connection between the development of the Tongs and the anti-Chinese climate in the late nineteenth and early twentieth centuries in America. Rose Lee argues that the Tongs resulted from the needs of a predominantly male ethnic community whose desires for rapid social advancement

---

[6] For a detailed discussion of the Chinese secret societies, consult Jean Cheneaux, *Secret Societies in China* (Ann Arbor: The University of Michigan Press), 1971.

[7] Readers who are interested in the Hung League and can read Chinese should consult David Lee, *A History of the Chinese in Canada* (Vancouver: The Chinese Voice), 1967.

[8] Lee, *A History of the Chinese in Canada*.

in America were blocked. Indeed, Tongs flourished during the decades following the "Chinese Exclusion" in 1884 and the Act of 1924 which made Chinese ineligible for naturalization.

As mentioned earlier, the two powerful Tongs in New York's Chinatown today are the On Leong Merchant Association and the Hip Sing Association. They are allegedly involved in illicit businesses such as gambling and prostitution. According to my informants, profits drawn from the illegal businesses have helped a few Chinese entrepreneurs launch legitimate enterprises. Chinatown insiders also maintain that the Tongs finance and support youth gangs, which are "hired" by the Tongs to "police" the streets in order to keep muggers away from Chinatown, to protect gambling dens operated by Tong members, and to cope with unruly gamblers.

THE NEW ASSOCIATIONS

The second, larger block of formal organizations are called the new associations, for they differ from the traditional associations in many respects. First, the new associations have been organized recently, and are not included within the umbrella of CCBA. Second, the new organizations recruited members from different social, economic, and educational backgrounds. Due to the influx of immigrants since 1965, the new associations have multiplied in size and number. New regional associations, alumni, political, commercial, and religious associations were established: for instance, the Taiwan Association; Hong Kong Student Association; Hing Wah Alumni Association; the Kwangtung Kuo-min University Alumni Association; the Lingnam University Alumni Association; the Taiwan University Alumni Association; and the Association for Progress. These associations have many highly educated members with cosmopolitan outlooks. Thus they differ markedly from the old sojourners who filled the rank and file of the traditional associations. At my last count (during my fieldwork in 1980), these associations numbered over 200 in New York City's Chinatown. The principal functions of most of these associations are social and recreational. Although all of them proclaim to protect the interests of Chinese Americans, these associations are generally apolitical, with three exceptions: the Association for Equal Employment for all Asians, the Organization of the Chinese Americans, and the Association for Progress, which are actively concerned with Chinese civil rights.

AGENCIES AND LABOR UNIONS

These organizations are oriented to the larger society and have their roots in the U.S. society. In fact, many of these organizations have direct connections with the government, churches, labor unions, and the nonprofit and charitable organizations, of the larger society. They serve as bridges between Chinatown and U.S. society. The emergence and proliferation of their social services were related to (a) the new resources available to the Chinese since 1965, including manpower and new funding available through the Economic Opportunity Act; (b) the consciousness of ethnicity; and (c) the multiplication of the new social problems as a result of the influx of the new immigrants since 1965.

Second generation Chinese who were raised and educated in the United States, many of whom were lawyers, businessmen, and social workers, realized they could tap resources from the city, state, and federal governments for the betterment of their ethnic group. They began to organize social agencies and to participate in organizations established by outsiders, such as the Community Service Society for community service. The more radical young Chinese-Americans, influenced by the Black and Puerto-Rican movements, and conscious of their own cultural heritage and the power of the People's Republic of China, returned from the suburbs to Chinatown to organize their people to fight against "oppression," and for equal opportunity and more funds for community services in Chinatown. In this way, these second generation Chinese-Americans were also brokers for the community.

Currently, the important social agencies are the Community Society Service; the Chinatown Advisory Council; and the Chinatown Foundation. The Chinatown Advisory Council was established in 1970 by Percy Sutton, Manhattan Borough President, and is made up of representatives from the government and from the schools, churches, and hospitals in the Chinatown area. This agency provides community services (housing, health, employment, education). The Chinatown Advisory Council also performs all the brokerage functions performed by the Chinese family, regional, and dialectic associations. The Chinatown Foundation was established by second generation Chinese-Americans with the intention of securing funds for all long-range service programs. Although these second generation Chinese do not receive salaries for their services, they are obviously interested in political power. Through their services they hope to gain the support of the people of Chinatown to compete for offices in the city's future elections.

According to my informants, the Office of Economic Opportunity has also funded some agencies with full-time, paid social workers to serve the people of Chinatown. The Chinatown Planning Council was founded in 1970 with funds allotted by the Office of Economic Opportunity and has been concerned with the problems of child care, youth, medical care, legal aid, and voter registration. Since the survival of this agency depends on the number of people it serves, officials have made an effort to draw a large clientele from the community.

These social workers want to be the principal brokers for the community, and they have made numerous attacks on the Chinese Consolidated Benevolent Association for its incompetence in obtaining necessary help for the poor in Chinatown. The CCBA counterattacked by claiming that the social service people exploit the Chinese people with their "altruistic" service. One of the kiu lings claimed: "These social workers are for their pockets." The point here is that some federally funded social agencies are competing with the traditional associations in recruiting clientele. There is much disagreement between the agency people and the leaders of the associations concerning the proper approach to social problems. Association leaders prefer to use peaceful means, such as letter writing, to gain assistance. Some of the newly organized community groups want to use more militant tactics, such as demonstrations and strikes.

CHINATOWN IN TRANSITION

From the "Chinese Exclusion" era to the present, Chinatown has made a series of structural adaptations. In the pre-1965 era, the various traditional associations dominated the social structure. As time went by, Chinatown developed new associations and absorbed new modes of modern bureaucratic organization such as agencies and labor unions. Traditional organizations, which were patterned after the rural social structure of traditional China, gradually found themselves unable to deal with the many contemporary social problems. The new immigrants who came from different social environments also encountered many problems in dealing with the old immigrants. Finally, the native-born Chinese-Americans and the bicultural, bilingual Chinese Americans, together with social workers, labor managers, and union organizers, started a new tier in the social structure. Present-day Chinatown in New York suffers not from underorganization, but overorganization. Each of the three clusters of social organizations in Chinatown attempts to serve the community, but via different routes. They compete with each other in terms of providing services and recruiting clientele. Their channels of communication are often blocked by subcultural differences and misunderstandings. The various groups of people in the community have diverse social experiences and drastic differences in the enculturation process. Some migrated from the rural areas of China, others from urban environments, and still others are from the U.S. The heterogeneity of the population is a contributing factor in the conflicts of the social structure. Another factor is change. Since 1965, Chinatown's population has diversified in terms of origin, marital status, age, sex, education, and occupations. The change in population effected changes in the goals of its members, in the kinds of social problems in existence, and in the perception of how to solve their problems. The new resources available also enable the establishment of the various new organizations, especially the social service agencies and the nonprofit charitable organizations. In New York's Chinatown, many of the functions that used to be performed by the traditional associations have now been taken over by the modernist social services providers, state funded agencies, or interest groups.

Generation gaps in the population also existed in the three clusters of the social structure. Community conflicts and segmentation, as pointed out by many anthropologists, are evident in many ethnic communities which develop quickly and have heterogeneous populations. Conflicts are thus part of the growing pains in the Chinese community of New York City. Another observation which seems to be relatively universal is the increased importance of the modern voluntary associations such as social service agencies, clubs, and labor unions.

3 / What kinds of people are there in Chinatown?

With advanced economic status in America, many ethnic enclaves disappeared and members of these ethnic groups were assimilated into the mainstream of American life. This was not the case with the Chinese enclave in New York City, whose population of 500 in the 1870s increased to 75,000 in 1980. The population in Chinatown is still growing with many immigrants joining it every day. Approximately 7 out of 12 Chinese immigrants who land in San Francisco will end up in New York City. What kinds of people are they? How do they rank and perceive each other socially? These questions will be answered in this chapter.

Some Chinese Americans have never lived in the Chinatowns nor have they had any connections with the ethnic enclave; these people are mostly students, visiting merchants, and government representatives from Taiwan, Hong Kong, or the People's Republic of China. They are in the country temporarily on various visas. Another group of non-Chinatown Chinese are the Chinese intellectuals who were caught in between the turmoil of the Civil War in China while studying in the U.S. during the 1940s. Some were professionals; others were employed in universities or business corporations. This group includes scholars, researchers, accountants, engineers, lawyers, and doctors. They tended to live among the White people. In an inclusive sense, they are part of the Chinese community, and some of them joined forces with the American-born Chinese to form The Organization of the Chinese Americans.

Those Chinese who live in the ethnic enclaves in San Francisco, New York City, Los Angeles, and Chicago are of socioeconomic backgrounds which require Chinatowns as "ports of entry," "stepping stones to the U.S. society," "places for business opportunities and employment," "places for permanent residence because of a familiar culture and language," "centers of social interaction because kinsmen and friends living in the area," or as "places to enculturate their children." Simply put, many Chinese-Americans need Chinatowns to survive. Within all the Chinatowns in the U.S., there is also a highly developed system of social stratification, with various models of "folk classifications" among the Chinatown residents themselves.

In New York's Chinatown, the natives perceive and categorize their social differences according to dialect, locality of origin, profession, prestige, time of arrival, lifestyle, degree of Americanization, attitude toward China, income, and age.[1] As with Chinatowns elsewhere, informants are hesitant to present a single system of stratification because there are many systems of stratification existing. One common system of viewing the social strata of the Chinese is to view the community as composed of the following: Old overseas Chinese (*Lou Hua Chiao* or *Lo Wa Kiu*),[2] new immigrants (*Sin Yu Min* or *San Yi Man*),[3] American-born Chinese (*Hua Yu* or *Wa Yeui*),[4] sailors (*Hai Yuen* or *Hoi Yin*),[5] and the boat people (*Nan Min* or *Nan Man*).[6]

Lo Wa Kiu (old Chinese) consist of foreign-born Chinese who came to the United States before 1965 and are now quite old. The majority came from the rural area of Kwangtung province, principally from the Sze Yup and Sam Yup districts. Although further subdivisions could be made among the old immigrants, they do share many things in common and, for the purpose of this book, it is possible to discuss them as a group. Moreover, the *San Yi Man* (new immigrants) and *Wa Yeui* (Chinese-Americans) tend to lump all old immigrants into one category and are antagonistic to them as a group. They call them peasants, backward, and conservative. New immigrants and Chinese-Americans contend that the old Chinese do not "know how to relax and enjoy life." The old immigrants retaliate by calling the *San Yi Man* (new immigrants) "westernized" and extravagant. They contend that they do not know how to raise children in a "good way" and attribute the increase of juvenile delinquency to the failure of family education among the new immigrants. The old immigrants call Chinese-Americans "*Juk Sing*," meaning useless, unyielding, and a group of people who have no roots either in China or in America, and consider themselves the "genuine" Chinese. They think they are more "Chinese" than either the Chinese-Americans or the new immigrants, and are concerned with preserving Chinese culture which they feel is "superior to the culture of the savage people everywhere."

Many old immigrants have accumulated some wealth through hard work and frugal living. They are usually in the typical businesses connected with Chinatown—laundries, Chop Suey Restaurants, groceries, and gift stores. They are older than new immigrants and Chinese-Americans. Another similarity among the *Lo Wa Kiu* is that they are active in and control all traditional Chinatown associations (family, regional, and village) as well as the Chinese Benevolent Association. Politically, they are anti-Communist and pro-Nationalist Taiwan.

Stuart Cattell (1970) referred to the old immigrants who hold leadership positions in the associations as the *power elite* of Chinatown. Not all old immigrants

---

[1] For a thorough discussion of the social stratification system in Chinatown, consult Bernard Wong, "Social Stratification, Adaptive Strategies and the Chinese Community of New York." *Urban Life*, 1976, 5(1):33–52.

[2] *Lou Hua Chiao* is the Mandarin pronunciation and *Lo Wa Kiu* is Cantonese pronunciation of the same term which refers to the Old Chinese immigrants.

[3] *Sin Yu Min* is Mandarin pronunciation and *Sun Yi Man* is Cantonese. Both refer to the new immigrants who arrived since the 1960s.

[4] *Hua Yu* is Mandarin pronunciation and *Wa Yeui* is Cantonese. These terms refer to the American-born children who have Chinese parentage.

[5] *Hai Yuen* is Mandarin and *Hoi Yin* is Cantonese pronunciation of the word "sailor." Generally, these terms refer to the jump-ship sailors.

[6] *Nan Min* is Mandarin and *Nan Man* is Cantonese pronunciation of refugees, or the "boat people" from Southeast Asia, who are principally of Chinese descent, from Vietnam.

are qualified for leadership positions; only those with wealth and connections can compete for these positions. And the only reward for holding a leadership position is prestige. Leaders are called *Kiu Ling* (leaders of the overseas Chinese), and they are the protectors and *patrons* of the less prosperous Chinese. Those who have not become economically successful are the leaders' *clients*. For a long time the unsuccessful *Lo Wa Kiu* refused to apply for welfare, even though they qualified for it. They preferred to live on their savings, take menial jobs, or live with their children. Only recently have some of them started to apply for welfare and use facilities provided for the aged by the larger society.

As a group of people, the *Lo Wa Kiu* are known for their proverbial frugality. They dress and live modestly. Even those who have made the grade economically live in less than comfortable houses. This is why the *San Yi Man* (new immigrants) and the *Wa Yeui* (Chinese-Americans) call the *Lo Wa Kiu* "hillbillies" who "do not know how to live." The old immigrants see no reason to assimilate into American society; on the contrary, they wish to maintain Chinese customs and the Chinese way of life in America.

The second group of people in this model of stratification is the *San Yi Man*, or new immigrants. These people came to this country in or around 1965, after the implementation of new immigration laws that abolished the national origins quota system. These new immigrants mostly come from the urban areas of China and have lived in Hong Kong for a time. They speak the Cantonese dialect used in Hong Kong or Canton and consider themselves more sophisticated, refined, urbanized, and "more genteel" than the *Lo Wa Kiu*. Generally, they came to the United States because: (a) they liked the material affluence of America; (b) they sought education opportunities for their children; and (c) they desired political stability. After finding a job and settling down their first desires usually were to learn how to drive and to purchase a used automobile. They dress better than the old immigrants, but they are still frugal in their lifestyle, and attempt to save a maximum amount of money by living in low-rent districts. There is more political apathy among these people; they do not adhere to the pro-Kuomintang ideology as do the old immigrants, but they are not pro-Communist either. This is understandable, since some of these new immigrants fled Communist China. They are not interested in the traditional family or regional associations in Chinatown. They want to achieve a double identity: They prefer to retain the Chinese way of dealing with one another, but they want to share the affluent American lifestyle and the education of the United States.

The new immigrants are involved in the garment industries and the new restaurants—Shanghai, Szechuan, and Peking as well as some modern Cantonese restaurants (see Chapter 4). Some are petty capitalists, owners of small firms. In terms of cash capital, the new immigrants have less economic power than the *Lo Wa Kiu*, although it is possible to find some new immigrants who can rival the *Lo Wa Kiu* in terms of property, income, and investments. As a group, the *San Yi Man* have a lower economic status than the *Lo Wa Kiu*.

The term *Wa Yeui* refers to Chinese who were born in the United States. Again, there are some differences among individuals in this group since it encompasses first, second, third, and fourth generation Chinese. However, they have many social characteristics in common and are lumped together by people in the community. The *Wa Yeui* generally are professionals employed by American firms. However, some lawyers, accountants, and doctors who speak the Chinese language do come to Chinatown to practice their professions. The *Wa Yeui* are more affluent than either the new or old immigrants. Few of them can speak the Chinese language or have Chinese-speaking friends, and they socialize mainly with members of their group or with American peers. This group is fully assimilated. They speak and curse in English and usually identify with Americans. As a group, they are sympathetic to the People's Republic of China and dislike Chiang-Ching Kuo's government. Recently, members of this group established a number of community service organizations in Chinatown with funds from different government agencies. Two frequent criticisms launched at this group by the *Lo Wa Kiu* and *San Yi Man* are that their consumption pattern is wasteful and extravagant and that they lack general knowledge of the language and culture of China. The *Lo Wa Kiu's* utmost dissatisfaction with the *Wa Yeui* is their "uncivilized" (non-Chinese) way of behaving. In terms of residence pattern they generally leave their parents when they become economically independent or marry.

The fourth group is the *Hoi Yin* (jump-ship sailors), China-born people from Taiwan or Hong Kong. After they jumped ship, they either got temporary employment as janitors from the different family or regional associations or from some Chinese restaurants. This group receives the least prestige and is ranked the lowest in the community. Their employers threaten to expose them to immigration officials if they do not abide by their employers' wishes. In order to get permanent resident status, some marry Puerto Rican or other Spanish-speaking women. *Hoi Yin* tend to socialize mostly with the new immigrants since they all speak Cantonese. They also share their attitudes toward the People's Republic of China and Taiwan and their consumption patterns.

The fifth group of people is called *Nan Man* and refers to the "boat people" who were expelled from Vietnam in 1978 and 1979. Many of the Vietnamese "boat people" are of Chinese descent and can therefore speak some Chinese dialect. Many of those who can speak Cantonese are able to find menial jobs in the business establishments in Chinatown as cooks, busboys, delivery persons, or janitors. Having suffered from adversity and hardship in Vietnam, and through their saga in the sea and in "refugee camps," many learned to abide temporary discomforts and are hard workers, busy rebuilding a stable life in America. This group of people provides a cheap labor pool which enables their employers to maximize their profits and enhance their aggrandizing activities with efficiency.

As a group, they are neither interested in community or world politics. The refugees are thankful for what they gained in the U.S. Their emotional connection with China is weak, since they were born and raised as citizens of Vietnam rather than China. Their hope is to achieve their "American Dream"—economic independence for themselves, education for their children, and a comfortable home base.

BIOGRAPHICAL SKETCHES

Case 1   Mr. C. Tam—Old Overseas Chinese

Mr. C. Tam is now a man of advanced age. His personal life history is representative of many of his generation of *Lo Wa Kiu* (or *Lou Hua Chiao* in Mandarin). As a man of age 86, Mr. Tam has been a resident of Chinatown for the past 70 years. As a teenager, he was sponsored by his brothers who ran a bean sprout and noodle factory in Chinatown. Immigration to the U.S. during the period from 1900 to 1920 was extremely difficult. After landing in San Francisco around 1900, Mr. Tam was held in an immigration detention center in the city for about a month awaiting interviews and other immigration routines. He was examined thoroughly by a medical staff and went through stringent immigration proceedings. The immigration officers also measured the distance between his lips and nose and the distance between his eyes for identification purposes. While immigrants from other nations were able to get their clearance in a matter of days, the Chinese had to stay in the detention center for a month. Immediately after he was cleared from immigration, he came to work as an apprentice in his brothers' factory, learning about the production of bean sprouts and noodles. He also went to Sunday school to learn English. The family factory was his business training center; as he gained proficiency as a factory worker for the trade, he was given more responsibilities and a salary. The factory at that time supplied restaurants in the various Chinatowns. As the business became more prosperous, he was made a partner in the firm with three other brothers managing the business. At age twenty-five, he returned to his home village to get married and sire a child. The marriage was prearranged by his parents in Toysan. Due to the "Chinese Exclusion Law" and other restrictive immigration laws, his wife and child had to remain in China for more than five years before they were reunited with him in America. The family business run by the brothers expanded, and he ran a daughter firm.

As a successful businessman, he was invited to join the various traditional associations. In fact, he was once the president of a powerful Tong. He related to me one Tong Wars episode in the 1920s:

> The Chinese just fought each other on the streets. One group of Chinese Tong members on one side of the street fired their pistols at the rival Tong members on the other side of the street in broad daylight. All the pedestrians, Chinese or non-Chinese, had to seek shelter in the stores nearby. Ordinary Chinatown residents were fearful of the Tong Wars. They normally would close their shops and stay at home upon hearing any rumors about any possible outbreak of Tong Wars in Chinatown. Only the members of the rival Tongs were killing each other. It is a sad story. Chinese killed Chinese. What a shame!

Mr. Tam also told me that in the old days the Chinese ran their daily affairs through the family name and other traditional associations. He was grateful for the help he had obtained from these associations:

> They gave me a lot of help. I celebrated festivals and all the Chinese holidays with my *Tung Heung Hing Dai* (brothers of the same village in China) in my

family name association. Before my wife and children joined me here, my family name association was my family. Some of the members, in fact, assisted me when I started my own firm. They gave me words of encouragement. Some of them worked for me like members of my own family. They worked hard and kept long hours. After I became successful, I repaid my family name association by donating money practically every month. The money was used for incense and oil (for ancestor worship) and other charitable purposes. Recognizing my contributions, I was made president of my own family association. I also contributed money to community activities in Chinatown, and was given "face" by the different associations. I was officer of many associations in Chinatown.

Mr. Tam confirmed that New York's Chinatown was relatively self-sufficient in the pre-1965 era. It was a community of "adult males" who ran their affairs through the traditional family name, regional, and other associations and Tongs. The Chinese lived in their own world in America; they had little or no contact with the larger society. Mr. Tam's factory supplied Chinese restaurants and grocery stores exclusively. And since he was in a Chinese business, he had no need to interact with outsiders. He has five children, all of whom are grown up; four of them are employed by American business corporations outside Chinatown, and one runs his business. He lamented the fact that his children are Americanized:

Raising children does not do any good in this country. They leave when they are grown up. I seldom see them nowadays, with the exception of my youngest son who is running the factory in Chinatown. They are too independent in this country! They are selfish, too!

Case 2   Mr. H.H. Lee—New Immigrant

Mr. H.H. Lee has an interesting life history. He was born in a French colony in southern China, and studied in a missionary school run by the French Catholic priests. During his college days, he studied accounting in Canton City. After graduation he stayed in Canton City until 1957, working in the accounting department of a big department store. As a Catholic, he suffered under the Communist regime from 1949 until his departure. He was interrogated numerous times by Communist cadres and was threatened with imprisonment. He believed that he could not practice his religion under Communism. Many of his colleagues who belonged to the same Catholic organization—the Legion of Mary—had been arrested and imprisoned in "labor camps." Mr. Lee believed that it was only a matter of time before he would be arrested, so he escaped to Hong Kong in 1957. Because of his facility in the French language and the help of a French Catholic priest, Mr. Lee was able to find a job in a French bank in Hong Kong. In 1959 he married the sister of a Chinese-American, and thus in 1969, he and his family were able to come to New York's Chinatown.

He told me that the early years after his arrival were very difficult. His wife worked as a seamstress and he worked as an auditor for a nonprofit organization. Every morning, he and his wife took their young children to the day-care center and then they went off to work. After the regular work day, Mr. Lee did some part-time work at home—bookkeeping for some small business firms and filing income tax returns. In fact, he taught his wife to help him with the part-time business. After three years of hard work, the Lee's bought a liquor store with their savings. At the same time, Mr. Lee took a real estate course and, in a year, got a license to sell real estate on the side. Also, knowing that the Chinese garment factory business was expanding and becoming a major business in the community as a result of the availability of cheap labor, Mr. Lee decided to run a supply shop servicing the sewing needs of the 300 garment factories in the area. As he was one of the pioneers in the supply business, he had very little competition and his company has prospered since its establishment in 1976. He sold his liquor store and used the proceeds to invest in real estate. Today Mr. Lee also owns several buildings.

Mr. Lee is one of the few successful entrepreneurs in Chinatown. Other new immigrants are not as lucky and are still working in grocery stores or the kitchens of the many Chinese restaurants. Mr. Lee's success can be attributed to a series of factors: (a) his know-how in business due to his training in business management; (b) his knack of seeing the opportunity and being quick to grasp it; and (c) his frugal and industrious lifestyle.

Mr. and Mrs. Lee now have three children who like other American-born Chinese children, would not like to pursue the business of their parents in Chinatown. All three seek professional careers.

Mr. Lee told me that he is a very busy person and that he is not interested in Chinatown's politics or in joining any of the traditional associations:

> I am not interested in having a name. I am interested in my work and in making money to support my family. I want my family to have a good life. I will retire after all my children are educated from college and have become professional people. That means that I need to continue to work hard for another 10 years!

Case 3 Mr. W.B. Chan—American-Born Chinese Professional

Mr. W.B. Chan was born in New York City. His father had a hand laundry store in Queens. Mr. Chan is a second generation Chinese-American. He said:

> We ABC (American-born Chinese) were ridiculed by the old immigrants as "Bamboo Stick" for not being able to speak Chinese and not being accepted as "white people." We are not here. We are not there. White people consider us to be inferior to the educated Chinese from China because we lack the "exotic value." This is the reason why many of us do not want to socialize with the China-born Chinese-American. We are different. Most of us are proud of the Chinese cultural heritage, but due to the pressure to assimilate and the lack of opportunity, we don't know much about the Chinese way. We don't understand the lifestyle of the new immigrants or the older generation. They like to speak Chinese and socialize only with their own kinds. We are discriminated against by the Chinese-speaking people in Chinatown and by the community's traditional associations. The CCBA said that we cannot hold offices as we are not "real Chinese." When I visited Hong Kong and Taiwan last year, my friends and I were treated as foreigners. When I went to eat with other ABC in New York's Chinatown, we were also treated as non-Chinese. The waiters are not very friendly and warm with us. I am an accountant working in a Wall Street firm. I came back here with some other ABCs to organize a community organization to assist the Chinese to receive welfare from the U.S. society. Chinatown is a

ghetto. People there are ignorant about the workings of American society. They don't understand the political system. The other day a senior citizen came here to ask me to help him get his social security check. Although he had worked in this country for more than 40 years, he has never collected any money from social security since his retirement three years ago.

Like Mr. Chan, other American-born Chinese are returning to the community to volunteer their services to assist the poor, the uneducated, and the aged. They want the community to participate in the resource distribution of the U.S. society in which the Chinese have contributed their labor and talents, their shares of social security and taxes.

Case 4   Mr. T. Hong—Jump-Ship Sailor

Mr. T. Hong was a jump-ship sailor. When he first went ashore in 1965, he sought help in Chinatown. He was fortunate enough to find a place to sleep in one of the regional association's headquarters, and to find a job as a dishwasher in a Chinese restaurant in Chinatown. He was paid $1.00 per hour with meals provided every day by the employer. He said:

The money was not good and the working hours were too long. One day I demanded to have more money, but the employer told me that he would inform the immigration office if I made more trouble. I kept quiet and worked until I found another job. In 1967, I got a job in a grocery store. Again, the employer took advantage of my illegal status. I had to do everything at any time the employer wanted me to do it. There were no fixed days off and no salary increase ever. The hours for work were not regular. I was frustrated and lonely. A friend of mine told me one day that I should get married to an American citizen and obtain a legal status. I got married to a Latin American woman who is a U.S. citizen. Now I have several children. I am now my own boss in the jewelry assembly business.

Mr. Hong is in the custom jewelry business, which he runs like a "cottage industry." He distributes the parts to be assembled at home by the housewives in Chinatown. After these jewelry items are assembled and finished, he collects them and then delivers the final products to the contractors or retail firms. He told me that there are just too many government regulations for a small businessman like him. "I have a lot of paper work to do and am dreadfully afraid of the sight of any bureaucrats. This is the reason why I have the front door of my office locked." While he is at work in his office, he always closes his door. Friends and workers who want to see him have to notify him in advance so that he can receive them at the front door.

Case 5   Mr. Trang—A Vietnamese Refugee

Mr. Trang is one of the Vietnamese "boat people" who arrived in 1979. Because he is of Chinese descent, he was mistreated by the Vietnamese Communists who threatened to send him to the "new economic zones" in the frontier region of South Vietnam. After donating a sizable number of "gold items" to the regime, he and his family were able to leave Vietnam. In addition to "buying the officials," Mr. Trang also had to give many ounces of gold to the skipper of his boat to smuggle him and his family out of Vietnam. They were picked up by the Malays and later sent to the U.S. He requested U.S. authority to relocate him and his family in New York City.

He has been working at many odd jobs since his relocation in New York City. All these jobs come from Chinatown's employers: He is a delivery man for a Chinese firm during the day; he washes dishes in a Chinatown restaurant at night; on Sundays he works as a handyman for Chinese families that need domestic help such as cleaning, painting, carpentry, or other odd jobs. Despite the busy work schedule, the hectic pace of life, and low pay, he is satisfied with his lot now. This is what he said about his life in America:

> After you are through with what I have been through, you probably will ap-
> preciate all these. At least, I have now my work, my family, and my freedom.
> I can buy anything I want to provided that I have the money. With hard work,
> I have now enough to buy food and clothing, to pay rent and afford eating out
> once a week in Chinatown's restaurants. I know I have to work harder than
> anyone, but in America, everyone works. At the beginning, it was very hard
> for me to work so many jobs. I am used to them now. By comparison to other
> refugees who live in camps in Southeast Asia, I consider myself lucky.

SUMMARY

Chinatown is heterogeneous, with peoples from all walks of life, ideologies, and lifestyles. From the biographical sketches of the old overseas Chinese to the Vietnam refugees of Chinese descent, we can catch a glimpse of the difference of social positions. Socioeconomic inequality and exploitation exists here as it does in all ghettos. Chinatown is no exception. The biographical sketches are by no means exhaustive and completely representative of all the people of New York's Chinatown. However, the residents of the community recognize five major layers in the social stratification of Chinatown. When they are asked to compare the stratification system of the Chinese in New York versus that of U.S. society in general, the members of the Chinese community believe that the vast majority occupy statuses corresponding to the lower and middle classes of the larger society. Some residents, such as some of the old overseas Chinese and new immigrants who own stores are ranked as middle class. The successful entrepreneurs who are wealthy are ranked as upper-middle class.[7] This group exists (with an annual income of $60,000) but is extremely small. The majority of the Chinese strive to be self-sufficient. They work long hours, and often they retain multiple positions or jobs. Still, a great bulk of the population subsists on the typical Chinese ethnic businesses (which will be discussed in Chapter 4).

---

[7] The very wealthy do not live in Chinatowns. *The New York Times* as well as the Chinatown newspapers have reported recently on the highly successful entrepreneurs and rich property owners in New York's Chinatown. A distinction must be made here. These are of Chinese descent but are not residents of Chinatown. For the most part, they are investors with money made elsewhere. Some are even citizens of the United Kingdom, Thailand, Malaysia, the Philippines, Taiwan, or elsewhere.

4/Making a living

The Chinese did not come from a nation of laundrymen or restauranteurs. Nor did they start these businesses immediately after they first arrived in the 1850s. Rather, these occupations are the result of their adaptation to the economic environment in the U.S. The Chinese who came to America in the nineteenth century were principally laborers who were engaged in railroad building, exploitation of mines, and clearance of farm lands in the western frontiers. Along the transcontinental railroad and the western frontiers, some Chinese restaurants were established, not as gourmet, luxurious enterprises, but as simple eateries to serve the Chinese laborers. Hand laundry shops were also established because there were no housewives or women to do this chore and, since laundry was always considered to be women's work, very few White men entered this trade. From the frontier days the Chinese learned that laundry is a low capital business with no competition from other White people. With some soap, scrubbing boards, and physical labor, a person could start his own business. The hand laundry soon captured the attention of other Chinese who were discriminated against in the job market immediately after the completion of the transcontinental railroad in the 1870s. Restaurants and laundry businesses have since been important ethnic enterprises for the Chinese.

The economic niche carved out for the Chinese continued to develop throughout the 130 years of their existence in America. In addition to restaurants and laundry, they opened garment factories, novelty and handicraft shops, and grocery stores, most of which were situated in Chinatown areas. In fact, this is an adaptive strategy in itself, because only in urban areas is it possible to get a large enough clientele for the Chinese type businesses. Second, with the mutual aid societies and protection associations, the Chinese can get assistance from each other. Third, until recently, there had not been an abundance of opportunity available to the Chinese. Many states had legislation against the employment of Chinese. In New York State alone, there were 26 occupations which the Chinese were prohibited from entering. These occupations included attorneys, physicians, bank directors, chauffeurs, dentists, embalmers, veterinarians, guides, liquor store owners, pawnbrokers, pilots, plumbers, horse track employees, watchmen, architects, CPAs, engineers, realtors, registered nurses, teachers, and others. This legislation was changed as recently as 1940. Fourth, many jobs need special skill, higher education, and a good command of the English language, traits which disqualify many new

37

immigrants and refugees. Fifth, there still exist many subtle discriminations against the Chinese in the area of employment. Some jobs require union membership, which often exclude the Chinese. The seniority system is in itself discriminatory. A minority group member is often the last to hire and first to fire. The Affirmative Action Program tends to favor Black men and women, so the Chinese are caught in the middle: They are not White and not Black. Finally, the lack of capital to launch an enterprise has also compelled the Chinese to stay in the ethnic niche. Thus, limited economic opportunity has driven the Chinese into Chinatowns and united them to protect a common interest.

Of the 432,000 Chinese Americans (U.S. census, 1970), 40 percent of the Chinese labor force are professionals, technical workers, and administrators. The rest are in Chinese type businesses: restaurants, garment factories, laundries, groceries, etc. Furthermore, one out of every three Chinese Americans is connected with Chinatown either by residence or by occupation. In New York's Chinatown, the ratio is even closer, with 50 percent of the 150,000 Chinese (1980) concentrated in the Chinatown area depending on the ethnic businesses for their livelihood.

CHINESE FOOD: FROM CHOP SUEY TO HUNAN CUISINES

Chinese restaurants have existed in the United States since the pioneer days, so the American public is familiar with Chinese food (see Figure 10). Compared to other national cuisine, Chinese food is usually cheaper. Also, Americans are fond of Chinese food because it is tasty and fastidiously prepared. In the Chinatown area of New York City, 5,000 Chinese work in 250 restaurants within five blocks.

Figure 10   A Chinese restaurant.

Outside Chinatown, the number of Chinese restaurants in the greater New York area probably totals approximately 4,500. They, too, draw their manpower from Manhattan's Chinatown. Restaurant workers commute daily to work in Chinese restaurants in Queens, Brooklyn, and the Long Island area.

The Chinese restaurant is the lifeline of many Chinese Americans. It not only supports many families, but also many would-be engineers, professors, and accountants. Also, the restaurants employ many Chinese college students who need money for their tuition and books. The Chinese restaurant in America is not a complete transplant of the Chinese restaurant in China. Many adaptations and innovations have been made. While the ethnic character of the business cannot be denied, many of the business items and practices have been adapted. Items like Chop Suey are favorites of the American diner, and fortune cookies, with their so-called "Confucius sayings," entertain many American diners after a Chinese meal. Because of the popularity of fortune cookies, factories have been established here to produce the "Confucius sayings" and "fortunes." And Chop Suey, as it is known here, is also a Chinese-American invention, which many visitors from China are not even familiar with.

Even in the restaurant trade, trend is important, and thus the success of the Chinese-American restaurant trade depends on its ability to follow the trend. Years ago the Cantonese Chop Suey dishes were adequate to satisfy the American diner. Today, with the publication of the Nixon–Chou En Lai banquet menu and other media events, many Americans are interested in experiencing other regional Chinese cuisines: Peking, Szechuan, and Hunan. The latest trend in American culinary taste is Hunan cuisine, and in order to meet the demands, many Chinese restaurants have to go Hunan style. Other considerations have to be taken into account before a Chinese restaurant can attract a steady flow of American customers. The decor must be comfortably oriental. The restaurants must have silverware (not just the chopsticks), and preferably a bar as well. While restaurants in China need only have tea, Chinese-American restaurants must also have soft drinks, ice, and cold water. For Americans who are not used to the hot spices, seasoning must be toned down to cater to the needs of the general public. For connoisseurs of Chinese food, there are specialty restaurants in Chinatown serving Dim Sum (Dien Sean in Mandarin), porridge, and noodle dishes. Thus, it is the ability of the Chinese restaurant to heed the culinary needs, trends and tastes that makes the restaurant business prosperous. Innovation, adaptation, and variety are essential parts of this ethnic business. Most recently, frozen Chinese vegetable Dim Sum and sausage dinners have attempted to capture the home cooking market.

Not only are Chinese restaurants a source of profit and income for a large number of restaurant owners and restaurant workers, they also have a positive effect on the overall economy of the Chinese in New York. Chinese vegetable farms in New Jersey and on Long Island have been quite prosperous because of continuous demands from Chinese restaurants. Trucking companies, Chinese grocery stores, noodle factories, construction companies, interior decorators, and import–export firms have also benefited from the Chinese restaurant trade. Thus the effect of the Chinese restaurant is deeply felt in the community.

LAUNDRY: FROM HAND LAUNDRY TO LAUNDROMAT

As mentioned before, Chinese hand laundries were originally established to serve the laborers of the railroad and the Americans who had no household help to do the laundry. As technology developed, laundry machines were invented, and these home laundry machines dealt a critical blow to the Chinese hand laundry business. The number of Chinese laundries dwindled down from 2700 in 1960 to 1000 in 1970. Today, of the remaining 1000 laundries, some have changed into laundromats and others have gone through reorganization, becoming washing plants or drying plants. Most of the stores in Manhattan are now merely collection and distribution stations. The hand laundry business, which used to be the largest Chinese business in America and supported many Chinese-Americans, is now labeled a "dying business." The owners were, for the most part, older, first generation immigrants (see Figure 11), some of whom died, returned to China, or retired. Many operators had to close down their shops because they failed to attract the second-generation Chinese-Americans and the new immigrants into the business.

Figure 11   A Chinese laundry.

THE GARMENT FACTORY: FROM SWEAT SHOPS TO THE ASSEMBLY LINE PRODUCTION

Technological change in American society also affects the so-called Chinese garment factories, which are actually assembly plants for American garment manufacturers. The garment factories are labor-intensive enterprises. As with the Jews, Puerto Ricans, and Italians before the Chinese, New York garment manufacturers distributed their materials, which had been selected and cut, to Chinese contractors to sew and assemble in their ethnic "sweatshops." Final products were returned to the manufacturers who then distributed them to the various merchants for wholesale and retail. The Chinese "sweat shops" have been expanded from 150 in 1970 to 300 in 1980, because of the (1) availability of manpower as a result of a large influx of immigrants in 1965; and (2) many Chinese seamstresses who prefer to work in the garment factories because they cannot speak English and because of the convenient location of the garment factories.

Although the pay in the garment factory is low, the work is not as regimented as in other modern assembly plants. People who work there tend to have face-to-face interaction. All are Chinese-speaking with familiar customs. Flexible schedules also allow many women to have time for their domestic chores and child care. Since the salary of a woman's husband is often inadequate to afford any modern amenities or even a comfortable living, she must work. In fact, in comparison to the rest of America, there are more working women among the Chinese-Americans (49.5 percent vs. 43.4 percent).[1] In Chinatown, the percentage of working women is even higher, around 80 percent (including part-time workers). The workers are paid by the piece, so their salaries depend on their skill and time invested. The average weekly pay is $150.

Some factories have attempted the assembly line method for the purposes of efficiency and productivity. As the experiment is still in an early stage, it is difficult to render any valuable assessment. Suffice it to say the garment factories are interested in innovation. They have even organized a "Garment Makers Association" in Chinatown to protect their interests; and the garment factory workers have learned that they must protect their interests too, and thus they have joined Local 23-25 of the International Ladies Garment Workers Union of New York City.

GIFT SHOPS AND GROCERY STORES: ETHNIC AND NONETHNIC CONSUMERS

Grocery stores are always an important business among all ethnic groups. Black, Spanish-speaking, as well as all Asian ethnic groups derive a substantial portion of their income from their grocery store receipts.[2] Another important Chinese

---

[1] This statistic is from the U.S. Census, 1970.

[2] This observation is verified by a study conducted by Charles Choy Wong. For further discussion of this matter, consult Charles Choy Wong, "Black and Chinese Grocery Stores in Los Angeles' Black Ghetto," *Urban Life*, 5:4 (January 1977), 439–464.

business is the gift shop, which depends entirely on tourism. Needless to say, almost all tourists are White Americans from all over the U.S. Both businesses increased their volume since 1965; The Immigration Law of 1965 stimulated rapid population growth in Chinatown. Now there are more people who look for business opportunities in grocery stores and gift shops. These two ethnic businesses require an expertise in Chinese culture, familiarity with tradesmen in various Chinatowns, connections with export and import firms in Taiwan, Hong Kong, China, and even Canada. Chinese grocery stores carry items such as squid, which is imported with the assistance of Chinese brokers from Canada. Canned octopus is imported from Mexico. Soy sauce, moon cakes, preserved fish, and other dry goods are imported from China, Hong Kong, and Taiwan (see Figure 12).

Arts and crafts are handled by knowledgeable Chinese merchants (see Figure 13). The mementos and souvenirs were purchased in far away places such as Tiensin, Peking, Shanghai, and were frequently purchased by importers in Hong Kong who, in turn, sold them to Chinese-American importers. Some items are directly ordered from overseas. The gift stores also supply the materials to decorate the Chinese restaurants. Thus, the customers of the Chinese gift shops are both the ethnic Chinese and the American public. Without the latter, no Chinese gift store can make a living.

Figure 12   A Chinese grocery store.

Figure 13   A Chinese novelty store.

The operation of the Chinese grocery store is highly complex. Some goods are first shipped from Hong Kong to Vancouver, and then on to Toronto. From Toronto, they are transferred to New York's Chinatown, where they are distributed locally and to Washington, D.C., Baltimore, and Boston. Part of the reason for the detour in the distribution of grocery items is the customs regulations. Some food items are not permitted to be brought into the U.S. but are permitted to be brought into Canada. Foodstuffs from Canada can be brought into the U.S. legally. Thus certain Chinese foods are finished in Canada and repackaged for shipment to the U.S. As for retail shoppers, New York's Chinatown is a distribution center for clientele from up-state New York, Connecticut, New Jersey, and the metropolitan area of New York City. Sunday in New York's Chinatown is full of people who come for recreation and shopping. Both restaurants and grocery stores are crowded with customers queuing up to spend their money. Friendship between China and the U.S. has made the American public curious about things Chinese. Certain items in Chinese gift shops have become fashionable: Americans are eager to own a Chinese quilted jacket, a silk blouse, a pair of shoes made of cloth. In the grocery stores, many white Americans are purchasing Tofu (soybean cake), bean sprouts, soy bean milk, soy sauce, pastry, lee chee nuts, cooking utensils (wok, rice cookers, steamers, etc.). There are about 60 to 70 stores of the two businesses. The prosperity of these businesses again reflects the changing attitudes of the larger society toward the Chinese and the ability of the Chinese-American to meet the demands of the public. This is also another case of "selling ethnicity" for a profit.

Chinese restaurants, laundries, garment factories, grocery stores, and gift shops constitute the ethnic niche of the Chinese. All of the above, in varying degrees are highly ethnic. With the exception of the garment factories, all of the businesses require ethnic expertise. The organization and development of the ethnic niche is a result of many years of trial-and-error experimentation, ingenuity, and hard work and is thus the outcome of a gradual process of adaptation to the economic environment of the U.S.

BUSINESS PRACTICES OF THE ETHNIC BUSINESS

Each of the ethnic businesses has its own idiosyncracies and, for that matter, there are differences from store to store within the same trade. They all share common characteristics to such an extent that they reflect cultural determinants. A presentation of ethnic factors in the business practices of the Chinese-American follows.

Kinship, Localities, and Business

Kinship, friendship, and locality ties are significant in Chinese culture. Kinship relations take precedent over all other human relationships. Friendship sometimes leads to quasikinship in that close friends normally become ritual-brothers, and thus are included in the kinship network (see Figure 14). Locality ties are important to the Chinese because China is composed of people who speak many

Figure 14   The Leung family association.

dialects. Therefore, similarity in the locality of origin facilitates communication due to similarities in local customs and dialect. In the American Chinatowns, immigrants were originally from places with strong lineage organizations. People who came from the same village were often related as descendents of a remote ancestor. Kinship, friendship, and locality ties were used for goal-seeking activities: emigrating, finding a house, obtaining employment, starting a business, etc. Many of the business firms in the pre-1965 era were started by brothers in partnerships. Partnership and employment extended to friends and people who came from the same region or people who had similar dialects or names. For this reason, certain Chinatowns are inhabited predominantly by people with certain surnames, from certain villages in China: Lees, Moys, and Chans are dominant in Chicago's Chinatown; Wongs, Chins, Engs, and Lees are common in New York's Chinatown. People from Pun Yee (or Pan Yu) control the Chinatown of Hanford, California; The Teng clan from Hui Ping (or Kaiping) is prominent in Phoenix, Arizona; and the butcher shops in the San Francisco Bay area are populated by people from Nam Hoi (or Nanhai).

In New York's Chinatown, many of the businesses could not have been started without support from kinsmen, friends, or people from the same village. Thus the Ling Kee Company was established by Mr. Chiu who was able to solicit a loan from his quasikinship circle—The "Four Brother's Association." Some of those in the Association are members of the same lineage in China, but the majority are not. The garment factory, Trans-Continental, was started by an older brother who borrowed the resources of his three sisters. Phoenix Bakery was a cooperative enterprise run by three brothers. Some Chinese cooperated with their in-laws, others with schoolmates. Capital formation on the basis of these informal social relationships is common even today in Chinatown.

Wui (Hui in Mandarin) is another traditional method of capital formation, one that is rooted in the home communities of the Chinese immigrants. Not everyone is allowed to participate in a Wui; only people with a relationship based upon kinship, friendship, associational connections, village mates, or class-mates will be accepted. It is a form of a rotating credit club, whereby members contribute a sum of money into a common pool. The highest bidder collects the pool and pays back to one member each month his contribution with interest. Thus, a member who collected the pool of $5000 from 20 members may have to pay $250 plus interest to each of the 20 members within a period of 20 months. *Wui* was instrumental in the establishment of many firms in the old days. Some forms of Wui persist in present-day Chinatown.

In the past racism precluded the Chinese from obtaining loans from the American banks. Recently, the Chinese-Americans were included as a minority group eligible to get business loans through the Small Business Administration and other federal agencies. However, there are many technical and legal difficulties that must be faced before Chinese businesses can borrow money from the banks. One is collateral; another is citizenship. Many of the Chinese who are permanent residents are not eligible. The 15 or so banks in New York's Chinatown are used principally for deposits. They are known as savings rather than loan institutions (see Figure 15).

Saving is a habit of the Chinese immigrants. After spending money for food, housing, and the daily needs of the family, the rest is saved to buy appliances, a house in the suburbs, to assist with the education of the children; in short, to achieve their American dreams. Some save for business purposes such as starting a firm, to invest in real estate, and to diversify one's business activities. In a five block area of New York's Chinatown, the number of banks is overwhelming (see Figures 15 and 16). These banks also do business transactions for the Chinese; such as overseas business drafts and remittance of money to relatives in Hong Kong or Taiwan.

Kinship and the Management of Firms

Kinship and its accompanying nepotism have been labeled by economists as obstacles for economic development. In the ethnic business of the Chinese, a common complaint is the lack of kinsmen and friends to assist in the development

Figure 15   This is one of the 15 banks in the five-block area of Chinatown, New York.

and expansion of the business. My research[3] in the developing countries also indicates that kinship plays a decisive role in the entrepreneurial activities of many businessmen. To start a small-scale family firm is the dream of many Chinese immigrants. Independence, profit, and being in control of one's employment and destiny are desirable attributes to which many Chinese aspire. By accumulating enough capital from many years of hard work and pooling all the savings from the family members, quite a few of the small-scale chop suey restaurants got started. Everyone who can work will work in the family firm. Wives and children usually get only what is needed for their daily necessities. Those who work in the firm have their meals together from the common kitchen. Eating together has several advantages: Manpower is saved because one person can do the cooking and shopping; and money is saved through the purchase of fewer costly items of equipment and by volume food purchases. Although family members can bring expenditures up for discussion, the decision is generally made by the family head. For example, before buying a family car the family would have a general consultation on the proper size, model, brand, and cost, but the family head would make the final decision and the payments. Day-to-day routine business operations are delegated to family members. Trust between family members provides security and support for the possible consequences of such decisions. A mistake by a son is

[3] I conducted a study on "Cultural Values and Economic Development in Singapore" in 1978. From interviews with many businessmen, I learned that family and kinship are crucial in the initial stage of economic development.

tolerated, and he will be given another chance since he learns from his mistakes (see Figure 17). Thus, this kind of family firm becomes a business training center for the family members.

Family firms are thought by the Chinese to be the most durable type of business. It generates family wealth, since everyone contributes to the family resources by savings, supplying free labor, and common expenditures.

The transactional behavior between father and children or family head and family members in the Chinese family firm is similar to that described earlier and that described by Benedict (1968). The father of the family firm is more than a father; he is a manager and a patron. To illustrate the process and operation of this kind of family firm, I will describe the Chan family and their family firm, Oriental Star.

Mr. Chan, Sr., the family head, founded the firm in 1968. Like many other new immigrants, Mr. Chan Sr. had to work as an employee for four years to observe and learn how to operate a restaurant. In order to avoid any misunderstanding and the breach of "friendship," he told his kinsmen shortly after his arrival in New York that he intended to work only for a couple of years.

After four years of work in the restaurant, he sponsored his family to come to the United States. In 1968, with the help of all the family members, he established a take-out Chinese restaurant. Mr. Chan now acts as the overall supervisor and treasurer, with the help of all the family members, and makes all the decisions because he is the only one who knows the restaurant business. His wife acts as

Figure 16   Manhattan Savings Bank in Chinatown, New York.

Figure 17   A family restaurant.

chief cook, and three of their sons assist her in the kitchen. One son is a delivery boy; another son does all the ordering and purchasing; and the third son assists his father at the store front.

Duties are rotated so that all the children have an equal opportunity to learn. All six children attended high schools in Hong Kong, but are not interested in furthering their education in the United States. Their ambitions mirror their father's: they wish to make money in the restaurant business by opening Chinese restaurants in the United States. After three years of hard work, one of the sons told me that the family firm is planning to open another restaurant and is in the process of selecting a location, preferably out of New York State, where they feel there are already too many Chinese restaurants. Each of the sons dreams of having his own restaurant someday. In fact, this ideal motivates them to pay attention to every detail of the restaurant operation.

Recently, the restaurant has been redecorated and a dining room has been provided for customers to eat at the restaurant. Mr. Chan is still the expert. He cooks, greets the customers, and establishes rapport with them. He also directs the kitchen staff. Thus, the father is a teacher from whom the children learn all aspects of the business: serving, bookkeeping, and cooking. Since there is no clear division of labor, each of the sons is expected to learn every aspect of the restaurant trade by working in the family firm. Mrs. Chan, however, is the permanent chef for the restaurant; she speaks little English, but cooks quite well. Those who work do not receive salaries, but draw what they need from the common fund for entertainment, education, and other necessities. In lieu of a salary, the father passes his knowledge on to his children, trains them to be successful restaurant owners, encourages them to start their own restaurants as soon as they can handle them, and promises all the financial support for such ventures. The eldest son is expected to head the new restaurant. When asked his feelings on being unsalaried, one son said: "We are all of the same family. The money of the family is ours. Why should we divide all the family wealth at the moment we need it to expand our business? We need the cooperation of all family members to build our future in this foreign land. Otherwise, we will be like those dogs who scavenge their own kind." Thus, family solidarity and the necessity of common fate for all members permeates the family firm environment. The father is now sponsoring more relatives from Hong Kong to assist with future expansion.

Another inducement for the children to stay in the restaurant trade is the realization that the Chinese restaurant is their ethnic niche. There simply are not many opportunities available to Chinese Americans, especially those who have recently arrived. As one of the sons said, "Where else can we excel? We have no high education. As you know, if you want to make a living as a Chinese in New York, you have to be in either the laundry, garment factory, or Chinese restaurant trade. As I see it, our future is in the restaurant trade as we have no training in the other two trades. People can do well in different professions and trades, and I believe that the Chinese restaurant really has a future for us."

Management and Size of Firms

Management in a Chinese firm is analogous to management in a Chinese family. Responsible positions such as managers, supervisors, cashiers, and chefs are filled by family members or kinsmen if at all possible. They are expected to work harder than outsiders. While it is difficult to demand an outsider to work extra time, family members are expected to do so just because it is the family's business. Second, the family firm may have to compete with other businesses in the same area. In order to stay in the business, the firm has to raise its profit margin by underpaying the family members and kinsmen for a time. In many of the family firms I visited, the family members simply do not draw any salary for their work during the lean seasons.

While it is true that some family firms succeed in running large-scale businesses, there is a shortage of kinsmen or family members to manage a firm, say, of 30 to 50 employees. Such firms are operated with the help of talented individuals who are loyal and willing to put up with the problems of the firm, the kind of individuals some employers refer to as "the right kinds of people." In some of the Chinese restaurants outside of Chinatown, White Americans are hired as waiters, bus boys, and kitchen aides. But the core group must be Chinese, because expertise in Chinese cooking is required and communication may be difficult with cooks who do not speak English at all. A bilingual staff is thus a necessity in many of the Chinese ethnic businesses.

Some of the operators of businesses have to deal mostly with Chinese-speaking employees. For example, in the jewelry assembly business Chinese contractors distribute all the jewelry items to Chinese housewives to assemble at home. This "cottage industry" keeps many housewives "employed" and at the same time allows them to attend to their domestic chores; they are willing to work for low pay because of the convenience.

The familial spirit also exists in the Chinese garment factory. Many seamstresses bring their young children to work. They also celebrate major holidays in the factory with their compatriots. After work, and on holidays, some of them may remain in the factory to play mah-jongg with their coworkers for recreation. In all the shops in Chinatown, New York, coworkers still address each other with kinship terminologies like "Guo (or Ge in Mandarin)" which means older brother, "Dai (or Di in Mandarin)" which means younger brother, "Bak (or Ba in Mandarin)" which means older uncle, "Suk (or Shu in Mandarin)" which means the younger uncle, "Sum (Shin in Mandarin)" which means aunt, etc. There is a certain amount of kinship and personal warmth in the environment of many Chinese firms. Disagreements and quarrels, nevertheless, still occur.

Exploitation seems to exist in all walks of life, including the confines of Chinatown. Typically, this occurs when an employer hires illegal immigrants, or new immigrants, who are unfamiliar with the new way of life in America. These immigrants are badly in need of money and, as other opportunities are denied them due to their circumstances and their lack of education and skill, these people are willing to work hard for low pay. I was told that the working conditions of the seamstresses are far better than those of restaurant workers. The former are mostly legal immigrants who are protected by the International Ladies Garment Workers Union. The restaurant workers still do not have their own union for all the Chinese workers in Chinatown. In 1980, progressive elements have attempted to organize a union in some of the larger Chinese restaurants. Initial success in one of the restaurants seems to indicate a union movement is in the offing.

Work, Work, Work

Restaurant workers have long working hours: 10–20 hours a day (see Figure 18). Some restaurants are open 24 hours a day, but have only two shifts. Further, the pay is not good. It is common for some employers to have tips figured in as part of the salary. At some establishments, tips are collected by the employers, and only a certain portion of the money is divided among the workers. At other restaurants, tips are collected entirely by the employers, and employees are paid a flat rate. Another aspect of the working condition is the business volume in the area. When customers are plentiful, especially during the weekends when Chinatown is crowded with tourists and shoppers, restaurants are very busy, and restaurant workers have no breaks whatsoever. The volume of work is unusually high.

Figure 18   Working in a Chinese restaurant.

Low pay, hard work, and long hours shatter the "American dreams" of many. All of these factors explain why the waiters in Chinatown are generally not cheerful. Some do get used to the schedule, and through hard work accumulate savings with which they eventually reward themselves with material things: stereo, automobile, electric appliances, even a house. Some even start their own restaurants. The hectic work schedule without many holidays is conducive to saving: no time to spend money. In two or three years, some workers could use their money to travel to Las Vegas or even Hong Kong. With their hard-earned money, many of the new immigrants go back to Hong Kong or Taiwan for a visit, and invite their friends out for picnics and dinner. Thus the image of the "Mountain of Gold" is perpetuated.

Other new immigrants who have to depend on the Chinese restaurant for their livelihood are disillusioned with the "land of opportunity." One worker told me that upon his arrival in New York's Chinatown he was disappointed by the old and poor housing conditions in Chinatown, the streets which always seem to be full of litter, and the "unhumanly" working schedule. He thought of returning to Hong Kong but did not want to disgrace his parents, who were still in Hong Kong, or to disappoint all those friends who saw him off at the Hong Kong airport and wished him well. Thus he decided to stay in America. He said:

> The first year was Hell. The second year was better because I got used to the lifestyle here. Now I enjoy it because I have been promoted to be a manager in the restaurant. I know that everyone is working hard like I do. I am no exception at all. I like the freedom here. Whenever possible, I take some vacation to travel either to Washington, D.C., Boston, or other places I have not seen.

Some restaurant workers are not this lucky. They change jobs frequently due to conflicts with coworkers or employers. All other doors seem closed to them because they have no other practical skills or, even if they do, they may not have the necessary language skills. As a result, some do return to Hong Kong for good.

Patterns of Authority Structure in Chinese Firms

Family, paternalism, and friendship play important roles in the Chinese ethnic businesses. As mentioned earlier, Chinese family and kinship structure focuses on the male. Kinship relationships are traced through the father's line. Authority is vested in the oldest effective male in the family, usually the father. When the father retires, the eldest son becomes the family head. Kinsmen from the father's side are given special preference in business ventures. Next in line for preferential treatment are the kinsmen from the mother's side. Maternal uncles and aunts are hired over other distant relatives and clansmen. Outside of the immediate kinship circles, people of the same village, friends, and people of the same dialect are considered for employment.

In the organization of firms, the same kind of preferential system follows. Typically, a Chinese will begin his firm with his nuclear family: wife and children. This type of family firm is prevalent in small-scale businesses: take-out chop suey restaurants; small grocery stores; newsstands; and small handicraft stores. Normally, after a period of years of hard work, and after having accumulated the necessary capital and basic knowledge of the business, the husband, sometimes with the assistance of the wife, will start to organize the firm. The husband, however, is the major decision-maker. The wife defers to him, although there is prior discussion and consultation between the couple. Young children, if there are any, will help out in the family business, according to their own capacities.

In the case of *Man Lee Chop Suey*, the eldest son is already 21. He has been assisting the family business since high-school days. His younger brother is 18. The husband and wife go to the restaurant in the morning to make all the preparations at 8 A.M. The restaurant is open from 11 A.M. till 10 P.M. The couple are chefs. The oldest son works in the store front as manager and cashier. He attends college part-time. He told me that his work is very demanding, as he must work from 11 A.M. to 11 P.M. every day. He cannot go to sleep right away because he needs some time to wind down, and early in the morning he goes to college. He realizes that it is nearly impossible to hold down a full-time job and go to college at the same time, and so he is contemplating "dropping out" and making the restaurant business his career. He said: "What is the use of going to college? After I finish my college I will not be able to find any lucrative job nowadays and will have to return to the restaurant. If I have to return to the restaurant I might as well stay where I am. Besides, my parents need me to manage the restaurant." His brother, who is now finishing his high school, works in the restaurant in the evenings, as a kitchen helper.

The operation of medium-sized restaurants and garment factories is more complex and more manpower is needed. Typically, the family head will be assisted by his wife, grown-up children, or in some cases by his brothers and sisters. Thus there is a core group of family members to run the business. Outsiders are also employed to assist. However, family members are given positions of responsibility; outsiders perform peripheral or routine duties. In the case of *The Chinese-American Restaurant*[4], the father is the head of the operation. He makes the decisions concerning where to get supplies, the menu, the numbers of outside helpers. He also delegates some power to his five sons in their areas of competence. One of the sons tends bar in the restaurant, and makes suggestions about decoration and about stock. The other son keeps the books and negotiates with the bank and credit companies about certain transactions. But ultimately, the father has to give final approval. His other three sons work in the kitchen as chefs. Three of his daughters-in-law wait tables. The restaurant business is the family business—no one takes it lightly. Outsiders are needed as busboys, dishwashers, delivery persons. When I interviewed one of these outside helpers, she told me the following:

> I have worked here as a delivery person for many months now. The Chinese people are very nice to me. They cook me meals although I was not told that free meals were included in my job. However, there are two parts in the restaurant. One is the family. The other group is the outsiders. They talk in their dialect to each other and have their inside jokes. They work in a particular way. No one takes a sit or takes a break to read the newspaper. They shift jobs and cover each other up. There is no strict specification of jobs. The father could be in here doing cooking or cleaning. He is also the cashier. The family eat their meals together. Their food is specially prepared and all sit around the table sharing their dishes.

The same operation is followed in a garment factory. Thus the owner of Eastern Continental is assisted by three sisters, each of whom supervises her section. As the garment factory follows an assembly line method, the three sisters are also familiar with all parts of the operation. They may switch jobs with each other to relieve boredom or to take over one another's duties when necessary. The older brother, who is the head of the firm, deals with the manufacturers to get the "bundle,"[5] after the garments are finished by his firm. He hires truckers to ship the final products to the manufacturers. He also makes decisions about "bidding"; he decides with which firm he will do business, which pattern or design he will accept, and the kinds of job orders he may take. He is in charge of the books and other business details. All the seamstresses are outsiders, hired from the Chinatown area. As is a practice in Chinatown, a good employer must attend to certain non-business aspects of the workers: He obtains information for his workers about school, immigration procedures, and insurance. He is their "patron." Thus, kinship, friendship, patron-client relationship, employer-employee relationships are intertwined in the Chinese firms. This seems to work well. The owner of the firm told me that if smooth interpersonal relationships are not maintained, the firm will be in trouble. Productivity will be low and there will be increased absenteeism. Eventually, rumors about it spread throughout Chinatown, and the firm will be unable to attract "good workers."

---

[4] This is a fictional name for the sake of anonymity.

[5] "Bundle" is garment contracting jargon for "the job order with all the parts designed and cut." All the cut works must be assembled by the contracting firms.

Whenever the husband's kin are available, they are sought for business activities. When these kinsmen are not available, it is customary for a Chinese to seek help and cooperation from his wife's kinsmen. The *Mandarin Restaurant*[6] in Chinatown is run by a 35-year-old man with capital from the parents-in-law. Like other medium-sized firms which cannot find a core group of kinsmen to assist in the day-to-day operation, the owner must hire a staff. In order to ensure smooth operation in the kitchen, the owner allows his chief cook to employ his own staff, from assistant cooks to busboys. In an effort to induce the loyalty of the chief cook and his staff, the owner of the *Mandarin Restaurant* made the former a partner in the business. This form of business operation, with the chef in the kitchen as a labor boss, is used to create a tighter operation and to maximize productivity and efficiency. Materials will not be wasted unnecessarily as the labor boss himself is technically a partner and his employees are his "clients" or "apprentices" or "younger brothers." The relationship is a form of patron-client relationship couched in a kinship-economic production unit.

In addition to family, kinship, and patron-client forms of business arrangement, the impersonal, large-scale business operation also exists in Chinatown. One example is the *Golden House*[7], which has a staff of 100 employees, and is organized as a corporation with many shareholders. There are also chain store operations. One example is the four restaurants run by a group of old overseas Chinese. Not all these corporations are well-managed. Some succeed and others fail. Many of the large-scale restaurants frequently change ownership. Reasons for failure vary from disagreements among owners to labor problems and embezzlement. According to Chinatown informants, size is a factor: When a restaurant increases its size without improving its managerial sophistication, it encounters the problems of accountability, cooperation, coordination, and impersonality, which eventually lead to the breakdown of the business.

In the past several years, thanks to the "floating capitals" from Taiwan, Hong Kong, and Southeast Asia and to the business wizards, some of Chinatown's businesses have assumed modern forms resembling highly successful American firms. These are newspaper firms with teletype machines, networks of worldwide distribution, and staffs of well-trained journalists and business managers. Some of the real estate firms and retail stores are well-organized too. This modern type of firm is rare in New York's Chinatown, but San Francisco's Chinatown has had more of these operations: the National Dollar Stores still successful today, China Mail Steamship Co., the Canton Bank of San Francisco.

While the new immigrants, old overseas Chinese, and Chinese-speaking businessmen rely heavily on the ethnic niche, second-generation Chinese-Americans have little interest in the ethnic businesses. There are some exceptions, such as the few enlightened and altruistic individuals who return to Chinatown to help community development and to act as "cultural brokers" to bridge the Chinese community with the larger society. Most of the second generation work as professionals with U.S. companies: lawyers, accountants, business managers, computer

---

[6] This is a fictional name for the sake of anonymity.
[7] This is a fictional name for the sake of anonymity.

scientists, and engineers. In the past several decades, discrimination against the Chinese-American has decreased, although subtle discrimination still exists. The employment trend for the native-born Chinese-Americans will continue in the professional areas. However, with new immigrants continuing to emigrate to the various Chinatowns from China and other overseas Chinese communities, the "ethnic niche" of the Chinese will likewise continue. Chinatown as an enclave will serve the emotional, economic and cultural needs of the first-generation immigrants. Chinatown will continue to serve as the "stepping stone," "the port of entry," "the residential area," "the enculturation unit," and "the economic zone" for the Chinese-Americans.

There are some successful enterprises, such as Wang Laboratories, Inc., the Sea King Corporation of New York City, and the Manhattan Fund, organized by Chinese-Americans, which had little to do with the ethnic enclaves; these enterprises were more connected with the larger society. Wang Laboratories was founded in 1951 in Tewksbury, Massachusetts, by a first-generation Chinese from Shanghai; the Manhattan Fund was organized on Wall Street in 1961 by Gerald Tsai, Jr.; and the Sea King Corporation (a shipping venture) was organized by an international shipping magnate from Hong Kong. The heads of these companies are international businessmen rather than ethnic entrepreneurs: They did not come from the Chinatown enclave, nor did they contribute to the community or the economy of the Chinatowns. These businesses are exceptional and not representative of the economic lot of the Chinese in America.

The Chinese-American Professionals

Nationally, the Chinese ethnic group contributes a solid corps of professionals to American society. According to the census of 1970, 26 percent of the Chinese in the continental U.S. are professional and technical workers. Another 8 percent are managers and administrators. The professional group is comprised of second-generation Chinese-Americans and Chinese students from Taiwan, Hong Kong, and China, who upon their graduation, remained in the U.S. Some outstanding professionals include C.N. Yang and T.D. Lee, who won the Nobel Prize in physics in 1957; C.H. Li, who was a recipient of the Albert Laiker Medical Research Award in 1962; Samuel Ting, who won the Nobel Prize for physics in 1976; T.Y. Lin, a reputable designer; I.M. Pei, an internationally known architect; James Wong Howe (1899–1976), a talented cinematographer; Dong Kingman, an artist; and Maxine Hong Kingston, an author. This list is by no means exhaustive.

Because of laws prohibiting Chinese-Americans from entering federal employment until the 1970s, there are relatively few Chinese working for the federal government. On the state and municipal level, there is a large number of Chinese clerical workers. Statistics (U.S. census, 1970) indicate that one out of six Chinese-American workers in the government bureaucracy is a low-level white-collar worker. These statistics should not confuse the economic picture of Chinese-Americans. More than half of them are still living in the ethnic enclaves, depending on the ethnic businesses for their livelihood. There are more unskilled than skilled Chinese-American workers. A large percentage (26 percent) of Chinese men work in service occupations in restaurants, laundries, and garment factories. And 43 percent of the Chinese make $4000 or less annually (U.S. census, 1970). Though Chinese rank higher than other ethnic groups in the white-collar and professional occupations (U.S. census, 1970), an economical and educational gap clearly exists among Chinese-Americans. While there is a sizable group of highly educated professionals, there is a much larger group of poorly educated people who work in the service occupations, and are the residents of the Chinese enclaves of the U.S.

SUMMARY

Chinatown's economy is shaped by the needs of the larger society and by the ability of the Chinese to meet these needs. Their ethnic niche has come about by historical factors and racism, as well as by adaptation on the part of the Chinese. The establishment of New York's Chinatown was triggered by anti-Chinese feelings in the West during the 1880s. The ethnic businesses and the various protective associations were efforts toward self-preservation and survival.

In the maintenance and operation of Chinese firms, the impact of traditional culture is apparent. Traditional family structure, old kinship practices, traditional friendship and patron-client networks are utilized. In contrast with the occupational structure of the second-generation Chinese-American, the ways of making a living reflect, perhaps, a transitional stage. One of these days, the native-born Chinese-Americans may be like the Chinese in Hawaii; likely to abandon the Chinatown economy. Meanwhile, Chinatown is a necessity for Chinese immigrants who cannot make a living outside Chinatown.

Availability of cheap labor and "capital" from overseas Chinese communities has created a surface prosperity in that the people who really benefit from the situation are "the owner-capitalists" who exploit the hard-working immigrants and are enriched because they pay low wages for quality labor. Thus, "Chinatowns" are an American phenomenon. Their social and economic structures are an adaptation to American life.

5/The Chinese family in the United States

In traditional China, one of the most important units of social organization is the family: Family is the focal point of one's life. Chinese philosophers and sages all moralized about the family. Confucius wrote extensively about the relations within the family: father-son, husband-wife, brother-brother. Solidarity and harmony within the family unit is emphasized. Social values and personal worth are often determined by reference to the maintenance, continuity, and functions of the family group.[1]

The traditional Chinese family can be characterized by five essential features which constitute the ideal. The first of these is the father-son relationship. Anthropologists have long noted the bond between the father and son in a Chinese family, which differs significantly from the stress placed on husband-wife relationships in American families.[2] This father-son relationship is the basis for "patriarchy, patrilocal residence after marriage, patrilineal descent, . . . and the inheritance of property by one or all legal (male) heirs"[3] (Lee 1963:272). As mentioned earlier, relatives are traced through the male line, and the authority structure in the family focuses upon the effective male figure, normally the father. After marriage, the bride moves into the household of the husband's father.

Family pride is another important value. In order to glorify one's ancestors, a man had to purchase property in his own home village. In dynastic days, men were encouraged to study for and pass the civil service exam to become a scholar-official; this position was ranked at the top of the traditional social structure. The man's success in the officialdom reflected not only upon his parents but also

---

[1] The Chinese family is a complete subject. Many sinologists have written extensively on the subject. Two comprehensive publications are: Maurice Friedman, "The Family in China, Past and Present," *Pacific Affairs*, 34 (1961): 323–336; Francis Hsu, "The Family in China," in *The Family*, Ruth N. Anshen, ed. (New York: Harper Brothers), 1949.

[2] For more information, consult Francis Hsu, *Americans and Chinese—Two Ways of Life*. (New York: Schuman, 1953).

[3] See Shu-Ching Lee, "China's Traditional Family, It's Characteristics and Disintegration," *American Sociological Review*, 18:272–280.

upon his own family and his ancestors. Likewise, an individual's disgrace brings disgrace to his family and ancestors.

The third characteristic of the Chinese family is the concept of the "big family," which entails many generations living under one roof. Since maintaining this "extended family" requires wealth, special efforts, and other pressures to stay together, many a time the extended family remains an ideal. Even though some attained enough wealth to organize a large family, these units often failed to stay together after the passing away of the patriarch. In fact, the average family size in traditional China was 5.3 persons per household.

Ancestor worship is another essential aspect of the Chinese family. Soul tablets are established at home as well as in the clan temples or ancestral halls. These tablets are wooden plaques about 14 inches high, 10 inches wide, on which the names of the ancestors and their wives are inscribed. These tablets are the focus of many ancestral rites. The long chains of ancestors are revered, and thus sons are considered so very important, for they carry on the family name and thus the ancestry.

Finally, the Chinese family is an economic unit, which owns common property —house, livestock, land, and other business assets. It is also a production unit, for the family often provides the labor for the family farm or family shop. Financial and labor resources are pooled together for economic purposes. The family is also a consumption unit, with a common kitchen that supplies food to all. Mutual sharing of prosperity and hardship give a sense of family solidarity.

The head of the family has the responsibility of seeing that the sons who are the legal heirs to family property and bear the family name, marry well, as continuity, stability, and perpetuation through generations must be safeguarded. This concern about continuity and stability gave rise to the practice of arranged marriages. Daughters, on the other hand, are raised to be "outsiders," and their status in the family is inferior to that of sons. They become members of the husband's lineage. The daughter's only family claim, if the family is well-to-do, is a dowry, which represents a fraction of the family's fortune. In the rural areas of traditional China (pre-1949 era), young daughters were sold as concubines or even prostitutes in times of extreme hardship.

The Chinese family is the foundation of Chinese culture. Values of harmony, propriety, seniority, industry, face, and frugality are imbued in the young. In the family, kinship terminology is used to distinguish age, sex, birth order, generation, and lineage, and authority is delegated accordingly. Senior generations are treated with respect. Older brothers have more power than younger brothers. Sons have more power than daughters. The eldest son's responsibility to the family is greater than the other sons'. Consequently, in the case of inheritance, he is usually given an extra portion to carry out his extra family responsibility: He must take care of his own family as well as his parents and his younger, unmarried siblings.

The Chinese family in America differs significantly from the Chinese family in China. Like other social institutions, the Chinese family underwent changes as a result of adaptation to the socioeconomic and political environments in the U.S. As these environments changed rather markedly after 1965, I tentatively discuss the Chinese family in relation to these two periods.

THE CHINESE FAMILY BEFORE 1965

As discussed before, few Chinese families lived in Chinatown prior to 1965 due to U.S. immigration policies and the cultural backgrounds of the immigrants. The majority of the early Chinese immigrants who came at the end of the nineteenth century and the beginning of this century wanted to make quick money and rejoin their families in China. They were the sojourners.

The Chinese Exclusion Act of 1882 and the Quota Act of 1924 made entry into the United States by Chinese wives very difficult. The Chinese Exclusion Act excluded all coolie laborers and made provision only for the entry of Chinese educators, students, officials, business owners, journalists, and other professionals. Few wives of early immigrants fit into these categories; thus the majority were not admissable to this country. The Immigration Act of 1924 ruled that alien wives were ineligible for citizenship and therefore were not permitted to enter the country. As mentioned earlier, many of the early immigrants were smuggled into the United States illegally, and were incapable of sponsoring their wives. And even if they entered legally, they were not citizens; the legislation of 1878 specifically denied naturalization to all alien-born Chinese.

According to the Bureau of Census statistics, out of 909 Chinese in New York State in 1880, only 12 were women. By 1890, when the Chinese population in New York State had increased to 2,935, only 33 were female. Male predominance persisted until 1965. For instance, in 1940 the sex ratio between Chinese male and female was almost six to one. The age group between twenty-five and fifty-nine years made up 73.4 percent of the total Chinese population (Wu 1958:24), and up to the end of World War II, New York's Chinatown was composed of adult, single males. Some authors referred to this as "bachelor society." Such labeling, although not inaccurate, is misleading, since the majority of this group were married, but their wives remained in China. According to Cheng-Tsu Wu (1958), in 1940, the ratio of married Chinese whose wives were not living in this country to those whose were living with them was six to one.

As mentioned earlier, the infusion of Chinese women into the population occurred in significant numbers only after World War II, with the implementation of the War Bride Bill and the G.I. Bill. According to Rose Lee (1960), up to the end of 1950 about 6000 foreign-born Chinese women, accompanied by 600 young babies, entered the United States under the War Bride Act. Half of these (3000) were believed to have settled in New York's Chinatown (Chu 1973). Even with the influx of Chinese war brides, the female and male ratio in 1950 was still far from even.

There are many different types of Chinese families. David Cheng (1948) has distinguished four types: the mutilated, where the husband was in the United States while the wife and children were in China; the grafted, where a Chinese man married an American woman; the divided, where the natural family composed of father, mother, and children existed; and the emancipated, where second-generation Chinese married.

Rose Hum Lee has also listed four basic family types: the early immigrant family, which came to the U.S. before 1924; the recent immigrant family, including war wives' families and reunited families; the stranded family, those of scholars, intellectuals, or officials who could not return to China; and the established family, second-, third-, or fourth-generation Chinese-Americans.

To give a succinct, yet comprehensive, view of Chinese families in the United States, I have distinguished four basic types of Chinese families: old immigrant families, including families which came before 1924 and war wives' families; Chinese-American families, including all second- and third-generation Chinese-American families; families of intellectuals, students, and officials who came to the United States before 1949 and were stranded in the United States and elected not to return to China because of the change in political regime; and new immigrant families, which came to the United States after the 1960s.

Among *old immigrant families*, both the parent-child and husband-wife relationships reflect Chinese family relationships of the Old World. The husband is the provider and head of the family, and the wife's activity sphere is at home. Although the wife is expected to assist with the husband's business, she has no interaction with customers or outsiders. In a laundry firm, for example, the husband usually mans the storefront while the wife assists behind the scenes by washing and pressing clothes. Also, there is a double standard regarding sex relations: A husband is allowed extramarital relations (R. Lee 1960:199), but a wife must be faithful. Having sons, the more the better, is very important for these families. Immigrant families retain the values of the Old World and filial piety is emphasized. Family authority is structured by age, sex, and birth rank. These families use traditional kinship terminology such as *Ko*[4] (older brother), *Dai*[5] (younger brother), *Che*[6] (older sister), and *Muy*[7] (younger sister). Boys are given more family authority than girls. The eldest son is the father's successor. The language used in the family is Chinese. All major traditional festivals, such as the Chinese New Year, the Moon-cake Festival, and the Dragon Boat Festival are celebrated. The perpetuation of the family business is usually entrusted to the eldest son. In fact, fathers often sponsored the immigration of their Chinese sons born on the mainland before they sponsored their wives. The idea was to ensure economic betterment for future generations by learning the family business and perpetuating it through the sons. Thus, many Chinese fathers wanted to start their sons in the family business while they were still young.

Both husband and wife are expected to maximize their savings through frugal living, but the wife in particular is expected to be a good housekeeper and spend little money. Frugality is highly valued among these families. Like the Chinese in the Philippines, Peru, and elsewhere, frugal living is the foundation of many entrepreneurial successes. Many of the older informants whom I interviewed constantly use the Chinese saying, "Kan Kim Hey Ka,"[8] which means "frugality is the beginning of success." Money saved is used for many purposes: (1) to

---

[4] "Ko" is Cantonese pronunciation. In Mandarin, it is pronounced as "Ge".
[5] "Dai" is Cantonese pronunciation. In Mandarin, it is pronounced as "Di".
[6] "Che" is Cantonese pronunciation. In Mandarin, it is pronounced as "Che" too.
[7] "Muy" is Cantonese pronunciation. In Mandarin, it is pronounced as "Mei".
[8] This is a Cantonese transliteration. In Mandarin, it is pronounced as "Chin Chien Chi Chia".

expand the business; (2) to buy real estate; (3) to buy gold and diamond jewelry, which is believed to have more stability than money and could readily be converted to cash; and (4) to send children back to China to receive a Chinese education and to get married.[9] Money is seldom deposited in the bank because these people lack knowledge and understanding about banking procedures and the English language.

The husband-wife relationship in the *Chinese-American families* differs significantly from that mentioned above. First, although the husband is expected to be the provider and the head of the family, he is no longer the undisputed decision-maker for the family. The husband is expected to consult his wife on major decisions, and frank discussions between the husband and wife are more prevalent than in the old immigrant families. The wife is often employed on her own. The measure of a successful marriage in the Chinese-American family is the absence of divorce (Lee 1960:245).

The consumption pattern of the Chinese-American family also differs from that of the old immigrant families. Thrift is not emphasized as much. Chinese-Americans spend more money on recreation, furnishings, automobiles, housing, and electrical appliances (Lee 1960). Even though some families have two wage-earners and an income that is often greater than that of old immigrant Chinese families, they do not have large amounts of savings or investments like the old immigrants (Lee 1960).

Attitudes toward children also differ in that Chinese-Americans are not obsessed with having sons; daughters are welcomed and treated equally (see Figure 19).

Figure 19   Chinese children.

[9] This practice was discontinued after 1949 after the Communists took over China.

Chinese-American families do not faithfully follow traditional Chinese customs. They eat Chinese food and celebrate some Chinese festivals, but they do not speak Chinese in the family. Although their parents might have been relatively interested in retaining some traditional practices, such as addressing each other with traditional kinship terminology, the children of these families prefer to follow the American way of addressing one another. There is more spontaneous discussion and communication in the Chinese-American families than in the immigrant families.

Children of immigrant families also encountered more adjustment problems than children of Chinese-American families. Immigrant children born in China were separated from their fathers for many years, and were brought up in a social environment that differed from that of their fathers. Thus, the generation gap was enormous and the father-son relationship in this kind of family was more strained:

> Teenage children meeting their fathers for the first time, and vice-versa, were numerous. Parent-child relations were often strained because each grew up and identified with a different social order—the fathers with the predominant Chinese-speaking sojourners' group and the children with the republican form of Chinese society. The latter had seen social changes occurring in swift succession, while the fathers had not. Although the fathers were anxious about their families' safety in China, they failed to comprehend children's fears, political leanings, social attitudes, desires for higher education, occupational mobility and relationships (R. Lee 1960:204).

Although this parent-child conflict did not exist among Chinese-American families, other conflicts did. From discussions with Chinese-Americans, I learned that second-generation Chinese were concerned with transmitting some knowledge about the Chinese cultural heritage to their American-born children. Their offspring, however, frequently wanted to be accepted by the larger society and were reluctant to learn the language and culture of China. In order to avoid conflict, an overwhelming majority of these parents compromised with their offspring and tried not to impose their preferences on them.

In Chinese-American families, the father is not the supreme authority; the mother also plays an important role in decision making. Children date whom they like and marry partners of their own choice. They also have freedom to select their own careers.

Children of the immigrant families were expected to take care of their parents in their old age, and it was customary in China for parents to live with the eldest son's family. However, in Chinese-American families, the children have more independence. Some even move out of their parent's homes as soon as they become financially independent.

Parents of the immigrant families were not interested in joining organizations like the PTA; lack of time and lack of proficiency in the English language prevented such participation. Chinese-American families, however, are quite active in the PTA (R. Lee 1960). This does not mean that the old immigrants were not interested in their children's education. They wanted their children to do well in school. Children were reminded that they could elevate their family status and glorify their ancestors by being good students.

Generally speaking, the immigrant families retained more Old World traditions than Chinese-American families, especially the Chinese language and interaction patterns within the family. Children of old immigrant families also kept closer connections to Chinatown and were more familiar with the socioeconomic life in Chinatown. Children of Chinese-Americans, on the other hand, are more acculturated and oriented toward the larger society and often become professionals employed by American establishments.

The *stranded families*, as originally termed by Rose Lee (1960), refer to the families of stranded students and intellectuals who came to the United States primarily to get an education or retraining, and were stranded as a result of the political situation in China in 1949. After the establishment of the People's Republic of China, many of these stranded families decided to stay in the U.S. These individuals tended to come from wealthier families in China and, as they originally came to the U.S. to further their education for the sake of social mobility in China, they were not concerned with Chinatown's community affairs. The Chinese ethnic enclaves, which were full of Chinese immigrants from southern China, had little in common with these "stranded individuals" and their families. They differed in social, economic, and educational backgrounds. In addition, there were differences in dialects, locality of origin, as well as orientation in the U.S. The "stranded families" lived mostly in the suburbs and cities among middle-class White Americans. Many of these intellectuals looked at Chinatowns with disdain. They felt that Chinatowns are not representative of China and considered the residents of Chinatown to be "low class" and "barbaric," since they were not highly educated and came from the southern regions of China. As most of the stranded individuals were professionals and came from northern China, they carried with them their regional ethnocentrism. For these reasons a "distance" existed between the stranded families and Chinatowns, until the 1970s when a change took place among these stranded individuals and their families. Part of the reason for the change of attitude was the awareness of ethnicity and the ethnic movement. Children and grandchildren of the stranded families, born in the U.S., became more democratic and equalitarian. The "class consciousness" and regional ethnocentrism of their parents or grandparents began to wear down, and some of these second- or third-generation Chinese-Americans even returned to the Chinatowns to organize community services for the poor and the needy.

The family heads of the stranded families possessed a higher degree of Westernization than the sojourner or old immigrant family heads. The former were also usually fluent in English and Mandarin. The second and third generation of the stranded families, however, are Americanized. Marriage is no longer by parental arrangement. Western "romantic" marriage, where courtship precedes marriage, has been adopted. In selecting mates, they are concerned with companionship, common interests, and mutual affection. Their attitudes toward sex, dating, marriage, and careers differ little from other Americans. Siblings are no longer required to address each other by reverential kinship terminologies. Although parental authority is still strong in the stranded Chinese families, there is more democracy in the family. Family meetings and discussions are also conducted formally and informally. The emphasis on father-son bond and the preference for son over daughter has disappeared, and equalization of the sexes within the family has occurred. The sense of family pride has been imbued in the children.

THE CHINESE FAMILY AFTER 1965

After 1965, the sex ratio among the Chinese in New York leveled off. Although the infusion of Chinese women began after 1945, it is only since 1965 that the proportion of male to female began to narrow.

One major reason for the change in the sex ratio is that after 1965 many new immigrants came to America with their families. New immigrant families have now joined the old immigrant families and the Chinese-American families in New York's Chinatown. This discussion will concentrate on the intrafamilial relationships of the *new immigrant families*. Unlike the old immigrant families, the new immigrant families want to make the United States their permanent home. However, from interviews and observations of new immigrant families, it is clear that the majority of the parents intend to instill in their children the traditional values of filial piety and teach them the Chinese language. At the same time, these parents want their children to learn the English language and receive college educations so that one day they may be *accepted* by the larger society. These parents hope their children will straddle both cultures—Chinese and American.

Although the husband is still expected to be the main provider, the wife also contributes to the common purse by working on her own or by assisting in the husband's business. Unlike the old immigrant families, where wives were expected to work either at home or within the family firm, wives of the new immigrants have no such limitations. If the husband has a firm, the wife usually helps him with it. Otherwise she may seek employment in one of the Chinese garment factories or restaurants. Some even work as cashiers or secretaries for Chinese firms in Chinatown.

The value of thrift is emphasized in the new immigrant families. Both husband and wife strive to save as much as possible by working longer hours to earn extra income and by living frugally. It is quite common for new immigrants to reside in rundown or substandard housing in order to cut down on rent. However, these people are quite generous with their food budgets: They are not stingy about spending money in Chinese restaurants or purchasing food for family consumption, because they believe one must maintain and improve one's health because it is the foundation of all gain-seeking activities. Extravagance in housing is not desirable because they believe that: (1) the rent in New York is far too high, especially for good housing; (2) expensive housing is not necessary because they spent most of their waking hours at work and use their apartments only at night to sleep; (3) it is better to save more money for a rainy day or for future investment or expansion of one's business than to use the money "unprofitably" for lodging; and (4) living conditions even in Chinatown, the Bronx, or some other inexpensive neighborhood were no worse than what they had encountered in Hong Kong.

The husband of the new immigrant family is the head of the family and the wife is the housekeeper, although she may also be employed outside the home. The husband, however, is expected to consult his wife on major decisions. Children are welcome regardless of sex, but most of the new immigrants prefer to have smaller families.

To most Chinese, family education means discipline by the father, and wives expect their husbands to do the disciplining. Some mothers blame the delinquency of their children on lack of parental supervision, especially the father's conspicuous absence from home during long working hours. Mothers believe that it is the father's place—as disciplinarian—to constantly "watch over" his children, particularly during the teenage and pre-teenage years, if the children are to turn out well.

The majority of the new immigrant parents are anxious to find good schools for their children (see Figure 20). On the other hand, they want their children to have some knowledge of the Chinese culture and language. Because new immigrants want their children to learn the Chinese language, many churches (see Figure 20) and the Chinese Benevolent Association run Chinese language schools on Saturdays, Sundays, and evenings so that Chinese children may attend both the public schools and the Chinese language schools. Although they do not verbalize this desire, most of the new immigrants want to establish dual cultural identities for their children. Some have succeeded in this endeavor; others have failed. Some children have great difficulty in the public schools because they are not proficient in English. They also find it difficult to attend two schools (Chinese and American) at the same time.

The new immigrant families differ significantly from the old immigrant families in their attitudes toward the larger society. The old immigrants always considered the United States a temporary place to live and planned to return to China as soon as they accumulated some wealth. The new immigrant families chose to emigrate to the United States of their own volition and intend to make it their permanent home. They seek two things: economic betterment and educational opportunities for their children, and they work long hours and live frugally to attain these goals. It is common for both parents to work six days a week.

Figure 20   A church-run school teaching both Chinese and English to the children of the immigrants.

They tell their children that their future education depends on the economic well-being of the family, and thus many children contribute to this goal by assisting in the family firm, in the hopes that the prosperity of the family business will enable them to pursue their future careers.

The new immigrant families speak the Chinese language, and the children address each other with Chinese kinship terms. Authority in the family is structured along age, sex, and birth rank. Parents are also concerned with instilling the sense of filial piety in their children and are quick to point out the evil of the American family system in which the young leave the old. Children are constantly reminded of their own potential helplessness in old age if they do not continue the Chinese family system. Parents instill certain values in their children: Yueng[10] (compromising spirit); yan[11] (tolerance); yang[12] (benevolence); lai[13] (propriety and politeness), wo[14] (peace). Again, this by no means suggests that the enculturation process was successful in all Chinese-immigrant families. New immigrant families that encountered the greatest difficulty in enculturation of their children are those with pre-teenagers and young teenagers, where both parents work full time. These children are known locally as Juk Kaks (Bamboo Joint), meaning hard and unyielding. Most juvenile delinquents[15] come from the group of teenagers born in mainland China, Taiwan, or Hong Kong, who were relatively young when they came to the States and had much difficulty adjusting to the American systems of schooling and living.

Once again, the new immigrant families hope their children will achieve two cultural identities: to speak Chinese and behave like Chinese, but to be accepted professionally as Americans. The old immigrant families were basically traditional and wanted their children to uphold all Chinese values. Chinese-Americans, especially the third generation, want to be accepted as Americans by the larger society. As Rose Hum Lee put it, the third-generation Chinese were for "integration," meaning the unreserved acceptance of the Chinese by the dominant group (Lee 1960:409).

I do not mean to imply that all new immigrant parents were so busy at work they never socialized with their children. It is customary for many Chinese seamstresses to visit their children in nearby grade schools, notably, the Transfiguration Church on Mott Street. They take them out to lunch in one of the nearby restaurants, and after lunch they accompany their children back to school. Many Chinese seamstresses work in the Chinese garment factories despite low pay just to be near their children's schools. Also, parents often take their children out to dinner, shopping, or for recreation. The restaurants in Chinatown are full of Chinese families dining together on Saturdays and Sundays.

---

[10] "Yueng" is Cantonese pronunciation. It is pronounced as "Yang" in Mandarin.
[11] "Yan" is Cantonese pronunciation. It is pronounced as "Jan" in Mandarin.
[12] "Yang" is Cantonese pronunciation. It is pronounced as "Jen" in Mandarin.
[13] "Lai" is Cantonese pronunciation. It is pronounced as "Li" in Mandarin.
[14] "Wo" is Cantonese pronunciation. It is pronounced as "Ho" in Mandarin.
[15] Although juvenile delinquency occurs in today's Chinatown, its frequency is far less than in other ethnic communities in New York and in the larger society.

SUMMARY

The immigration of the Chinese to America in the past 120 years was characterized by periods of various degrees of restriction, exclusion, and relaxation. The types of family that developed in the U.S. had a great deal to do with the immigration policies. Family life and experience were not comparable among all the Chinese in America, not even among the second- and third-generation Chinese-Americans. Some were raised in old immigrant families, some in the new immigrant families, others in stranded families, and still others in Chinese-American families (both parents are American-born). The common feature among them is pride in the family. Whether or not they live in Chinatowns, they want to establish families, have children, and help their children to obtain higher education. Children were encouraged to study and do well in school. Parents in general attempted to give moral as well as financial support. Children at a young age were taught by the elders to be diligent at school (see Figure 21). I have seen children of new immigrant families study by their mother's work stool in the garment factory, or read their books while their mothers visit and pray at the Buddhist Temple or work in the family store.

On Sundays, many parents from Chinatown, New York, as well as outside of Chinatown, take their young children to the Chinese school run by the CCBA to learn Chinese. Among them are children of the new immigrants, Chinese-Americans, and old immigrant families. While their children attend the Chinese school, the parents socialize with each other in the Chinese restaurants: sipping tea and eating their lunch.

Some of the parents are so concerned about inculcating Chinese culture in their children that they compel them to go to the Chinese school every day after public school. I was told by many parents that they succeed only with children who are younger than 10, for as they grow older, they lose interest in the Chinese school, partially due to academic pressure, and particularly due to lack of time and pressure from their peers to participate in the "melting pot" to be Americanized.

Figure 21   Graduation Day: Education is highly valued in the community.

"School dropouts," and youth gangs exist in all Chinatowns.[16] There are many factors contributing to school dropouts and the activities of youth gangs. First, is the economic hardship which requires both parents to work long hours away from home. They may not have any time for their children, and do not know what their children are doing. Another factor is that of adjustment. Without parental support, teachers' understanding, and positive encouragement and assistance, many youngsters cannot cope with rapid changes in their life. In America, they are not familiar enough with the English language, and Chinatown, New York is no less alien to these newly arrived immigrant children. Lack of academic preparation and peer group pressures are also factors in "dropping out." Of all the factors discussed, the most important of all is the lack of family attention of some new immigrant families.

Of the four major types of Chinese families, three are prevalent in today's Chinatown: (1) the old immigrant families; (2) the Chinese-American families; and (3) the new immigrant families. In addition to being an economic center, Chinatown is also an enculturation center, transmitting basic Chinese values and molding the character of the young Chinese. It is an ethnic enclave in which the residents learn about the American culture, conduct their economic activities, interact with their compatriots, practice their customs, and transmit the ethnic heritage to the young.[17]

YOUTH GANGS—A WAY OF LIFE

Chinatown had been lauded as a "model community," one without juvenile delinquency. One of the reasons why this was true in the pre-1965 era was the simple fact that there were few juveniles around in any of the Chinatowns. In such a predominantly adult male society, any youths who were present tended to participate in adult events. Similarly, in the pre-1965 era, the few juveniles and youths in their early twenties participated in criminal behavior along with adults. These young people were labeled by the American public as "hatchetmen," "hatchet boys," or "high binders." Information about them was confined to the Chinatown community. Members of the community kept silent about these activities, as most of the Chinese in China or the U.S. did not wish to involve the police or outsiders. "Thou shall not wash thy dirty linens in front of strangers" was the hallmark of many older immigrants. Others feared reprisals and kept silent. Traditionally, law and order in the community was enforced by the Chinese family. As indicated earlier, the phenomenon of gangs arose due to family problems and educational problems: Ill-prepared students tended to drop out. Also, lack of opportunity for Chinese youths and the availability of monetary reserve to gang members contributed to the problem. The Tongs have been patrons to these

---

[16] More discussion on this subject will appear in Chapter 6 of this book.

[17] I must hasten to qualify that New York's Chinatown is in the process of culture change: it is more than just an ethnic enclave and has recently acquired some characteristics of an "interest group." (This concept will be discussed further in the next chapter.)

youth gangs, because they needed them as "muscle-men" to control the unruly gamblers and maintain order in their gambling establishments. Gangs could be seen roaming the streets of Chinatown as early as the 1940s, due to the relaxation of immigration laws. Toward the end of 1945, about 1000 youths were admitted to the U.S. with one parent. It did not take them long to become frustrated by the social reality of the Chinatowns. Their "American dreams" were shattered before they started their new lives. They were expected to do many of the menial or unskilled jobs, such as dishwashing or laundry because they lacked skill in English. This was an abrupt comedown for these youths who, in China, were considered to be well-to-do and were treated with respect from their countrymen. Upon arrival here, there was a decline in status. Meanwhile, society promised many material rewards such as cars, clothes, movies, and recreation to those who had money. Thus motivated, many of these youth joined the gangs and participated in other criminal activities: auto thefts, burglaries, etc. The situation deteriorated further after 1965 with the influx of larger numbers of young people from Hong Kong.

Many scholars believe that the gang phenomenon is typically American. They argue that Chinese youth, exposed to the process of Americanization and the conflicting values of East and West, have to follow the inevitable path that the Irish, Italian, Puerto Rican, and Black children went through.

Present-day street gangs in San Francisco and New York have grown in numbers and in variety of criminal activities. They are into homicide, robbery, extortion, and purse-snatching. In New York's Chinatown, gangs were trained in the martial arts by the Tongs and sent to protect their illegal gambling establishments, and to watch for muggers from other groups. Some of the gang members were specifically assigned to keep out "bullies" and "ruffians." An informant told me that he was already a member of a secret society in Hong Kong, and because of his background, he was invited to join a youth gang. While he was on assignment, he could collect "expenses" from the Tongs, which averaged $200.00 per week. Once, he and his group were reimbursed for travel and rewarded with bonuses for their visit to Boston's Chinatown to give a "lesson" to a group (a black gang) of repeatedly unruly customers of a Chinese restaurant. They fought the group with valour and were given a victory celebration party.

The youth gangs do not always take orders from the elders of the Tongs. Members of the gangs practice extortion, vandalize business property, engage in power struggles among themselves, rob guests of the restaurants, including the Chinese guests attending banquets and other festivities, and mug movie-goers by simply asking their victims to deposit their wallets and jewelry into a bag. Now, with better educational backgrounds among the new immigrants, more of the gangs' activities are reported to the police.

Chinatown's fifth precinct now has a Chinese police officer and several detectives who specialize in gangs. I was told that they are still short on manpower, as there are many gang members now. One of the police officers told me that there are about 500 gang members. Of these, 250 are active members belonging to several factions: the Flying Dragons, Ching Yu, White Eagles, and Black Eagles. The major Tongs backing these gangs are On Leong, Hip Sing, and Tung On. The On Leong Association is organized nationally with branches in

Boston, Chicago, Miami, and Houston. Its protégés—the Ghost Shadows—sometimes appear in the Chinatowns of these cities, and in New York they control the territory east of Mott Street. Flying Dragons are active on Pell Street and Bowery.

Present-day street gangs in New York's Chinatown include not only foreign-born Chinese, but also native-born groups. Many are recruited because they are promised the companionship of pretty girls, fancy cars, and money. They are promised excitement and happy times, and the guaranteed backing of the Tongs— "Nothing would go wrong. If things go wrong and you are jailed, you will be bailed out in no time. Even if you are convicted, your record will be wiped clean after age 16." The legal system unintentionally condones the activities of the gangs because of leniency applied to juveniles. For this reason, some gang members went so far as to commit murder.

Case 1   The Knifing of Mr. M.B. Lee

M.B. Lee is a successful, modern businessman in Chinatown. An owner of a Chinese restaurant and a bakery, Mr. Lee participated in many community activities, such as officer of the Chinese Chamber of Commerce, Jaycees, and CCBA. When he was the president of CCBA in 1977, he launched a campaign to fight the gangs. He rallied the community in support of the police. He even went as far as to the Manhattan district attorney to testify and demand that stiff bail be set against the leader of the Ghost Shadows, who was arrested for assault. For his courageous action, he was stabbed by a member of the gang. Mr. Lee was severely injured but managed to survive. The youth pleaded guilty to attempted murder and is now in prison.

Case 2   Murder of a Gang Member

The members of the gangs frequently have to fight for their territorial imperatives as well as to control their rank and file. All members have to take the oath of secrecy. Violation means death. One of the members wanted to go "straight." He cooperated with the police and provided information about his gang. He was killed with five bullets: one for each eye, one for each ear, and one for the mouth. It is supposedly a warning for any "turncoats" and the community.

Despite intimidation from the youth gangs, a community effort was organized. The police have added staff, including a Chinese translator, to work on the "Chinatown Project" in the fifth precinct. There are three bilingual staffers. The various community organizations are developing programs to assist the young people. The CCBA had coordinated two community demonstrations to keep the fifth precinct. The community organization with the assistance of the police have launched a program to educate and encourage the public to make complaints and report crimes about juvenile gangs and other illegal activities.

The numbers of the gangs have increased since 1965. Against an increased population of Chinatown, however, the percentage of juvenile activities is relatively small (see Tables 1 and 2). One point should be emphasized: Juvenile

TABLE 1   CHINESE GANG-RELATED ARRESTS BY CRIME IN NEW YORK CITY'S
FIFTH POLICE PRECINCT: 1975–1978 (CHINATOWN)

Crime	1975	1976	1977	1978
Murder & Attempted Murder	1	37	5	1
Possession of Weapons	19	38	7	15
Assaults	21	13	2	11
Extortion	0	12	13	10
Robberies	14	27	32	9
Burglaries	9	27	0	5
Rapes	15	0	0	0
Other	6	17	15	17
Total	85	171	74	68

Source: New York City Police Department, Fifth Precinct.

TABLE 2   NEW YORK CITY'S CHINESE POPULATION

	In the metropolitan area	In Chinatown area (estimates)
1950	18,404	13,697
1960	32,831	20,761
1970	69,324	40,000
1980	150,000	75,000

problems do not originate from all types of Chinese families; gang members tend to come from certain types of families, mostly from new immigrant families and some from Chinese-American families.

I do not mean to imply that these families cause juvenile delinquency. But most gang members come from families with both parents at work with little interaction among their members or regular family life. Thus, the economic condition of the new immigrants and their way of life in America are principal reasons for parental neglect. One of the informants told me his family story:

I came with three children to the U.S. seven years ago. My oldest son was then 9 years old. His Chinese education was superior to many of his peers in China-town. But his English was weak. I knew that he had a hard time in school, but I had reprimanded him many times and asked him to get "good grades." My wife and I do not know anything about his school work, so we cannot help him with his school work. Nor do I know how he did in school. He is the only person who knows English in the family. He paid bills for us and signed for us his report cards. There might be letters sent to us from school, but I don't know. I don't read English. My wife works in a factory from nine to five. I work irregular hours even on Sundays and holidays. I seldom see my son although we all live in the house. We have different hours of sleeping and work. I was told recently by my relatives that my son is a gang member. When I knew it I reprimanded him. He ran away from home and I have not seen him for days.

Economic hardship of the new immigrants in the ethnic enclaves is an obstacle to stable family life. Proportionately, the majority of the Chinese, including the immigrants, are concerned with the well-being of their children. A close-knit integrated family with mutual respect and order is desired by all family heads, with the education of the children utmost in their minds. In fact, this is one of the reasons why they migrated to America.

Newspapers and the mass media often mislead the public by comparing Chinese youth gangs to the Mafia or the vicious Triad Society of Hong Kong, which is an organized criminal gang. In fact, the youth gangs differ from these organizations in many respects. First, the present-day Chinatown youth gangs are teenagers, "school drop-outs." Deprived of parental care, spurned by White and other ethnic groups as a result of stereotypes, many school-age children make themselves easy prey to the evil forces in society. The gangs in Chinatown are not highly organized. Dissension exists between and within gangs. Many gang members outgrow their gang as they become older. In fact, many of the former gang members become good citizens and are employees or social workers in Chinatown. Further, once they are no longer teenagers, they are under pressure to go straight. Gossip and moral sanction actually force many of them to find ordinary employment and become respectable members of the community. Also gangs in Chinatown seldom bother tourists or innocent bystanders. In fact, they never "mug" tourists or the ordinary people in the street.

Some of the former gang members who made good told me that it was a "good way" of life for them at that age. They could write expense accounts and get "advances" and "reimbursements" from their bosses. Being a gang member also gave them a sense of belonging and a sense of power. One point must be emphasized: Gang members are not supported and accepted by the community as a whole, just by a small group of people who are in the illicit businesses. Youth gangs are a special adaptation to the environment, and a temporary way of life for some teenagers in Chinatown. Had better alternatives been available to them, they might not have had to resort to the "criminal way" of life. From conversations with informants in Chinatown, the consensus is that the "system" ultimately creates the "gang phenomena." Here is one typical statement about the youth gang:

> Society fails to attract these youngsters to school. The education system fails to provide the necessary instruction to improve their English and keep them in school. What the educational system fails to do is not remedied by the economic system either. They could not get any decent jobs anywhere in New York except in Chinatown as busboys and dishwashers or gang members. Sure, some people need the gangs to make a lot of money. It pays to be a gang member. What is there to lose? If you are a gang member, you are protected. When you are arrested, you will be bailed out.

6/Ethnic identity of
Chinese Americans

The Chinese in America have had identity crises for many years. As an ethnic minority, the Chinese operate under a series of constraints imposed on them from their host society in the New World as well as from their mother country in the Old World. Although other ethnic communities in the U.S. also have to deal with both the host and the mother countries, the significant difference is that the Chinese came from a culture which for centuries considered itself to be technologically and morally "advanced." The Chinese migrated to the U.S. only recently when China was undergoing political and economic change. Economically, China became an underdeveloped country since the Industrial Revolution. Politically, China changed from an Imperial dynasty to a republic. After the overthrow of the Manchu dynasty in 1911, the Chinese republic was troubled by civil wars and the power struggle between the Communists and the Kuomintang (KMT for short, referring to the Nationalists). The internal politics and political troubles at home indeed interfered with the ethnic identification of the Chinese in America.

Life in the New World was not without its share of hardship. The anti-Chinese campaign in the late nineteenth century, the social and economic discrimination against the Chinese—both blatant and subtle—in the early twentieth century, and the favorable change of attitudes toward the Chinese and other ethnic groups all affected the identity search of Chinese Americans.

Chinatowns, U.S.A. are not all alike. They differ from each other in size and in historical development. Some are situated in large metropolitan areas, like New York, Chicago, Philadelphia, San Francisco, Los Angeles, and Boston. Others are located in smaller cities, like Memphis, Tucson, Sacramento, Detroit, and El Paso. Although there are basic similarities in social structure and occupational specialization within each Chinatown, the population is not homogeneous. In New York's Chinatown, the population structure of the community is a result of a complex historical process—U.S. immigration policies, international events and U.S.–China diplomatic relations. The question of ethnic identity can be understood only in the context of the social structure as well as the economic adaptation of the various Chinese population groups in the community. New York's Chinatown now has five major groups who differ in social, and economic backgrounds, as well as lifestyles and degrees of assimilation. These groups are the *old overseas Chinese, American-born Chinese-American and naturalized Chinese-American, new immigrants, jump-ship sailors and refugees,* and *disenchanted/disenfranchized youth.* Each of these groups has its own philosophy about its destiny in the New World, and the different interpretations of the Chinese ethnic identity sometimes conflict with each other.

SOJOURNERS AND CHINESE CULTURE IN AMERICA

The old overseas Chinese (Lo Wah Kiu)[1] are the older immigrants who came to the U.S. before 1965. They are the first generation, foreign-born Chinese who got into the U.S. by virtue of kinship or friendship relations. Their sponsors—family, kinsmen, or friends—were plagued by social and economic discrimination. The old overseas Chinese, as well as their predecessors, had witnessed or even suffered from the various forms of discrimination in American life. Their goal in this country was to improve their economic lot and accumulate enough wealth to resume life in China at a later date. With this goal firmly implanted in their minds, they were able to put up with any *temporary* adversities and short-term injustice in America. While they lived in the New World, they looked forward to returning to their homeland. Sociologist Paul Siu[2] called this the "sojourner" mentality, and their ethnic identity is *Overseas Chinese.* They practice traditional customs, observe traditional Chinese holidays and festivals, and follow the social interaction pattern of the Old World. In dealing with each other, they emphasize kinship, friendship, and other informal social relations, such as similarities in the village of origin, dialects, and writing of the surname. The old fabrics of social network relations are used for goal-seeking activities: finding housing, obtaining employment, mediating disputes, securing mutual assistance. They live a life separated from the mainstream of American life. Their contacts with White Americans occur only in the contexts of their ethnic businesses: restaurants, laundries, etc. Due in part to their low educational background and the nature of their work (which does not require a good command of the English language), the sojourners had little or no communication with the larger society. They live, work, and socialize in the areas of Chinatown. The loneliness of the sojourners who had no families in the U.S. does not require elaboration, and in response to it there arose illegal gambling dens for the recreation of the Chinese.

Some of the sojourners in New York's Chinatown still have their immediate families in Hong Kong or China, and some of them sponsored their families to America since 1945. Not only did the sojourners come from different social and economic backgrounds, but they also differed from other Chinese subgroups in lifestyle, emotional needs, and in attitudes toward assimilation. The sojourners came from the Sze Yup, Sam Yup districts, and spoke a similar dialect called Toysanese. They were known to be the strong supporters of the Republican Revolution led by Dr. Sun Yat-Sen. The overseas Chinese, including those in America, contributed morally and financially to the 1911 revolt in China to over-

[1] This is Cantonese pronunciation; the Mandarin pronunciation is Lo Hua Chiao.
[2] See Paul Siu's "The Sojourner," *American Journal of Sociology,* July 1952:34–44.

throw the Manchu dynasty. After the establishment of the Republic of China, some of the sojourners returned to China to join their families and enjoy their retirement. But despite the success of the revolution of 1911, the economic malaise in traditional China continued. Though immigration to the U.S. was halted for the Chinese, they still flocked to this country by legal or illegal means. Even during the Chinese Exclusion Era (1882–1943), young Chinese were admitted to the United States under student status, and Chinese merchants were admitted as well. Their children were also permitted to come into the U.S. Other Chinese entered the U.S. illegally.

Although the course of migration to the U.S. was difficult, after arriving in this country seldom did the sojourners intend to stay forever. In the post-1945 era, China emerged as one of the five major powers (China, U.S., Great Britain, France, and Soviet Union). The sojourners were proud of the achievements of their home country. Victory parades were conducted in all Chinatowns, closer ties were maintained with the Chinese government which at that time was the Nationalist Government (or KMT). When the hostilities between the KMT and the Chinese Communists arose, many of the sojourners sided with the nationalists. After the communist take-over of China in 1949 and the outbreak of the Korean War in 1954, the KMT used Americans' fear of communism to gain substantial control of the community. The sojourners often claimed that they were the symbols of Free China, and they are. In addition to being oriented to Chinese culture in their lifestyles, the sojourners living here during the period from 1945–1972 are basically pro-KMT (see Figure 22). President Nixon's visit to Peking in 1972 marked a new era of Chinese-American relations and created a feeling of pride among many Chinese. Many of the sojourners in New York's Chinatown today are still oriented toward China. On the surface the old overseas Chinese seem to be sympathetic toward the KMT. However, the *Lo Wah Kiu* (leaders of CCBA and other traditional organizations) may profess support for the KMT in Taiwan but may also be sympathetic toward the People's Republic of China. From my fieldwork research in the past several years, I believe that the old overseas Chinese have no intention of returning to China. They identify principally with Chinese culture rather than Chinese politics. Nor are they ready to assimilate. They are isolationists who prefer to live in Chinatown to pursue their economic goals through the ethnic businesses. Those who have leadership qualities still enthusiastically participate in the traditional district, village, hometown, and dialect associations. They are unfamiliar with the political processes of the U.S. and are still fearful of the larger society. Even in the community, the leaders of the Chinese language school are not seeking help from the larger society for fear of losing community control.

The Lo Wah Kiu still cling to the Old World mode of living, and many are convinced that they will never be treated equally by the larger society. After all, they reason, this is not our "real" country. This feeling of rejection is understandable only if one has lived the life of a "sojourner" in America. Prior to their departure from China, the sojourners viewed the U.S. as a "mountain of gold." After their arrival, however, when they worked as laborers and performed many menial jobs in American society as busboys, laundrymen, grocery store clerks,

Figure 22   A traditional association is displaying both the American and the Kuomintang's Chinese flags.

garment factory workers, waiters, domestic servants, they discovered that due to racial characteristics they did not receive equal treatment. Although the sojourners were basically *apolitical*, they were labeled as "Communists," "Fifth Column." Having lived in an era of intense racism, the *old overseas Chinese* think any intimate contacts with the larger society will invite trouble, since competition with the White laborers in the past led to anti-Chinese feelings in California, the passage of the "Chinese Exclusion Law," the exclusion of the Chinese from more than 27 jobs in New York State. Stringent immigration procedures were adopted to screen Chinese immigrants including the use of the Bertilon System, which was originally used by French prisons to identify their inmates. Since Chinese people look alike to Americans, this humiliating system measures the distance between the eyes, and between the mouth and nose. Chinese were often singled out for discriminatory treatment by American laws. In California, laws were passed in 1882 to exclude Chinese from public schools, and in 1883 to prohibit Chinese from testifying in court. Other states had similar anti-Chinese laws. In addition to legal discrimination, there was social discrimination. One older immigrant told me that when he was drafted to serve in the Air Force in the 1940s, no one wanted to room with him. In the past two decades, many discriminatory laws have been abandoned and replaced by laws in favor of minority groups.

The attitudes of many of the old immigrants have not changed much. As one of them said:

> Now that things have changed for the better, why ask any more! Do you know that we could have been put in the concentration camp during the Korean War? They did that to the Japanese during World War II! Remember, we are not White people and have no power in this country. What we can do is to show the goodness of our "culture" and our civilized way of behavior. See how they all come to view our New Year parades and enjoy seeing our exotic costumes. As long as the American comes to Chinatown to spend money to support our livelihood and not discriminate against us like they did in the past, that is enough!

The Lo Wah Kiu prefer to be left alone to go about their traditional way of making a living. In the 1960s, a group of young Chinese in Chinatown were demonstrating against the American tourists for their sightseeing activities. The radical American-born Chinese students felt that sightseeing was an insult to the Chinese for they "look at the Chinese as if they are in the zoo." This attitude of the radical students is opposite that of the old immigrants, who like to take up the stereotypical Chinese manner, for they feel it helps them make a living. Thus behaving and speaking in a Chinese manner is an adaptive strategy too. In sum, there are ideological, practical, and circumstantial reasons for the *old overseas Chinese* to adopt the identity of a "real Chinese." The components of this "real Chinese identity" include embracing the traditional lifestyle, identifying with "Free China" or Taiwan, and adopting traditional symbols and manners.

In the past, identifying with Taiwan had many advantages. In so doing, one avoided being labeled a communist, and gained much prestige. Leaders of the *old overseas* were invited to visit Taiwan and were decorated by high-ranking officials in Taiwan. In addition, pro-Taiwan Chinese community leaders often got better value on export/import merchandise and were able to obtain permits and visas for business activities more readily. I must also mention that some *old overseas Chinese* also suffered from the revolutionary activities of the Chinese communists. Their relatives, and sometimes even they themselves suffered from the various purges, land-reform, and other movements in China. Some had been imprisoned and later had the opportunity to escape to America. These old immigrants, needless to say, are anti-Communist.

As mentioned before, common to all the *old overseas Chinese* is their orientation toward Chinese culture and their willingness to isolate themselves from the mainstream of American life. Living in ghetto-like Chinatown, they are in America, but exist as Chinese. This ghetto-like environment gives them a sense of separation. They read only the Chinese newspaper, listen to Chinese music, eat Chinese foods, and socialize with other Chinese. They are highly ethnocentric and see no worthwhile reason to assimilate into American society. To these old immigrants, Chinatown is a sanctuary, a residential neighborhood, an economic zone, and a place to practice their traditional culture. The ethnic organizations are intended to act as catalysts for the practice of Chinese culture and mutual aid. Life for the old immigrants is basically China-centered.

It is not purely for ideological reasons that the old overseas Chinese insist on identifying with China and Chinese culture. Isolation of the Chinese community

from the larger society also enables the old immigrants who are successful entrepreneurs to exploit the labor resources in Chinatown. Many Chinese, who are
unable to find jobs in the larger society due to lack of connection with it, are forced
to accept less-than-minimum wages for their work in Chinatown. Therefore,
economic and political expedience, as well as discriminatory experiences of the
past and lack of English language skill, all influence the Chinese to stay in Chinatown and embrace the "Chinese ethnic" identity in America.

CHINESE-AMERICAN IDENTITY

Another subgroup within New York's Chinatown are the Chinese-Americans,
including native-born Chinese-Americans and foreign-born Chinese, who are
citizens of the U.S. The native-born Chinese are citizens by the principle of *jus
solis*; the foreign-born obtained their citizenship by naturalization. The U.S. Supreme
Court ruled that a person born in the U.S. of Chinese parents is of American na-
tionality by birth. New York's Chinatown today has second, third, fourth, and
even fifth generation native-born Chinese Americans. With regard to naturalization, there have been many rulings prohibiting the Chinese from being naturalized
citizens, on the assumption that the Chinese would not make good citizens because
they are a different race and come from a despotic nation. The Exclusion Law of
1882, the Immigration Act of 1924, prohibited alien Chinese from becoming
citizens. These laws were repealed in 1943 and since then many Chinese have
applied for naturalization. These Chinese citizens, whether by birth or by naturalization, have recently developed a new ethnic identity, which is sometimes referred
to as the American-Chinese identity, at other times as the Chinese-American
identity. Within this group, a distinction about birth place is made. Socially, there
seems to be some distance between the American-born and the foreign-born
Chinese. The American-born Chinese have little knowledge of Chinese culture or
language; the foreign-born Chinese feel superior to the American-born since they
are bilingual and bicultural and come from a different socioeconomic strata.
Sociologist Rose Lee noted this phenomenon in her book, *Chinese in the United
States of America*:

> The most common manifestation of identification reaction is verbalization, as,
> for example, calling the American-Chinese "low class," or "chop suey people."
> By so doing they hope to carry favour with, and achieve acclaim for, the dominant
> group (Lee 1960:112).

As time goes by, however, the differences between these two groups of Chinese-
American citizens will diminish. They constitute a solid professional group and
have similar aspirations. They want to be accepted totally into the larger society
and are willing to fight for equal treatment in American life. Although they are
citizens of the U.S., they had for years been treated like second-class citizens, although the situation has changed markedly in the past several years. Because they
possess distinctive racial features, they are often treated differently by the larger
society. One American-born Chinese informant told me the following:

My parents run a Chinese restaurant. They were from the Old World 40 years ago and speak mostly Chinese at home and at the restaurant. Their lifestyle is Chinese-culture oriented. But I was born in the U.S. 27 years ago. I grew up with other White Americans and was educated in grade school, high school, college, and medical school in this country. I know more about the history, culture, and language of the U.S. and have thought that I am no different than other White Americans. Now that I am out of school practicing my profession as a physician, I definitely feel that people treat me like an ethnic and a member of another racial group. I am reminded that I am Chinese although my orientation and lifestyle are more American than Chinese. I have little knowledge about Chinese history, language, or culture. I am a U.S. citizen. Yet I am treated as if I am not equal to other Americans.

Thanks to the emphasis of higher education in Chinese culture, American-born Chinese were sent to college. As a result, these American-born Chinese (also known as *Wa Yeoy*) normally work as professionals—as doctors, accountants, engineers, lawyers, etc.—in American establishments. Yet they are made conscious of their racial and ethnic heritage by the larger society.

The naturalized Chinese-Americans came from different social origins, mostly from middle-class or well-to-do families. In the past, they made an effort to distinguish themselves from the Chinatown population and the American-born. Strictly speaking, they were not Chinatown's constituents, since they did not reside there. They felt superior to the residents of Chinatown on account of differences in social origin and educational background. The foreign-born naturalized Chinese came to the U.S. in the 1940s. Some of them were the "stranded students and intellectuals" who originally intended to stay in the U.S. for a short period of time to complete their education or specialized training. As a result of civil war on China's mainland and the subsequent takeover of the Chinese Communists in the old country, these students or intellectuals were forced to abandon their hopes of returning to China and to live and work in the U.S. They subsequently readjusted their visas and became citizens. After many years of work and experience, many of them learned about the racial prejudice against the Chinese and the working of American democracy. Keenly aware of their ethnic and cultural heritage, they shared many identity problems with the American-born Chinese. In order to fight racism and to be treated equally, both the American-born and foreign-born Chinese-American citizens believed that they had to join forces. Inspired by many other ethnic movements in the late 1960s and 1970s, principally the Black and Chicano movements, these two groups of Chinese-American citizens began to feel that in order to be treated equally they had to stand up for their civil rights, participate in American politics, and form effective organizations to fight racism and to change the image of the larger society toward the Chinese in America. Some of them returned to Chinatown to organize the community and to offer voluntary social services. It has indeed been an uphill battle, but the process of forming an interest or pressure group on behalf of the Chinese has been initiated. While the ultimate goal is for equal opportunity and equal treatment, the immediate goals are not often agreed upon by all Chinese-Americans. Some want to instill ethnic pride by emphasizing their contribution to U.S. society. Others believe that they have to organize the community into an ethnic solidarity group to participate in resource distribution. They want to get their share from the city, state, and federal government. Others want to emphasize the plight of the Chinese-American to gain sympathy from the larger society. Mr. Irving Chin, a Chinese-American lawyer, commenting on the relationship between the Chinese-American and U.S. society, had this to say:

> Many Americans and non-Chinese are looking at us and saying very smugly and with a certain amount of irony, "It looks like you're just one of us: you're having problems too." What they don't realize is that thousands of people have been brought into the U.S., left to settle in a small area and not given any financial support. That's not fair. We are being discriminated against in terms of funding. . . . Some people say that the Chinese are a very silent minority—they never speak up. But we've been speaking up for the past year and a half and have been getting a few deaf ears. It seems to me that the stereotype of the silent Chinese is not only not of our making but is perpetuated by those who prefer to have this image cast to prevent us from getting our rightful funding (*Bridge Magazine*, 1971, *1* (2):17).

Irving Chin is an American-born Chinese-American who has returned to New York's Chinatown to lend a helping hand. Other foreign-born Chinese-Americans, who feel subtle discrimination in the larger society, want to assist the less privileged Chinese residents in New York's Chinatown in obtaining the financial aid that other minority groups have acquired. Both the American-born and foreign-born Chinese-Americans feel that the American public views the Chinese people as a homogeneous group and do not recognize the difference between the Chinatown Chinese and the middle-class Chinese-Americans living in the suburbs. Attorney Irving Chin said:

> The American bureaucracy doesn't recognize us as a minority group. We haven't made it yet. We're not second-class citizens, we're third-class minorities. Students who apply for scholarships specified for minorities are told, "I'm sorry, you can't apply. You're Chinese, you're not a minority." . . . We are American taxpayers and our dollars go to the American government. We are therefore entitled to have our share of educational funding (*Bridge Magazine*, 1971, *1* (2):17–18).

The Chinese-Americans are willing to press for their fair share in resource distribution. Both the American-born and the foreign-born Chinese-American have come of age and realize the importance of becoming an integral part of the American system. They have launched various community programs in Chinatown, educating the residents about the meaning of ethnic identity, the importance of participating in the political process, the contribution of the Chinese-American to American life, and their fair share of resource distribution in the U.S. Through consciousness raising and united action, this group of citizens of Chinese descent hope to transform the ghetto community into an ethnic power capable of fighting for its well-being as an ethnic group.

As a result of the catalyst work of the Chinese-American, many more social agencies and community organizations have been established to serve the emotional, physical and housing needs of the community. Confucius Plaza, the stay of the Fifth Precinct, the establishment of the various community clinics, and the senior citizens centers are some of the results of the activities of the collective efforts of the Chinese-American community workers.

The demarcation line between the American-born Chinese-American and foreign-born Chinese-American has been reduced recently. From my field research in 1971, 1977, and 1980 I noticed that many of the modern community organizations are staffed jointly by American-born and foreign-born Chinese. Also the Organization for Chinese-Americans accepts both native-born and foreign-born citizens and permanent residents. These members have similar goals, fears, and aspirations. They want to be treated equally—like other White Americans. After all, the U.S. is their permanent home. They are also concerned with their civil rights and their acceptance by the larger society. They have little or no interest in the politics of China or Taiwan, nor do they identify themselves with these countries. Since the emergence of the People's Republic of China as a world power, and especially after the U.S.–China normalization of 1972, some Chinese-Americans are taking more pride in their Chinese heritage. However, their allegiance is to the U.S. The Organization of Chinese-Americans expressly indicates that it has nothing to do with politics in any foreign country. They are American first, and this takes precedence over membership in any other Chinese ethnic group. When traveling overseas or visiting China, Chinese-Americans always consider themselves citizens of the United States of America. And thus they demand to be accepted as equals by the larger society.

MULTIPLE IDENTITY OF THE NEW IMMIGRANTS

The new immigrants that settled in New York's Chinatown refer principally to those Chinese who arrived in this country after 1965. These new immigrants were admitted according to a system of preference—priority was given to spouses, children of U.S. citizens, specially skilled personnel, and brothers and sisters of citizens or refugees. As a result of the 1965 immigration law, Chinese were eligible to enter the country in significantly larger numbers. Shortly before the enactment of the 1965 immigration law, some Chinese were admitted to this country by virtue of the Refugee Act of 1953, which was later amended and expired at the end of 1956. In New York's Chinatown, all those immigrants admitted since 1953 have been labeled as *Sun Yee Man* (new immigrants). Their influx into the community produced significant changes in the demographic composition. For the first time, the ratio between Chinese males and females became more equal. In general, the educational backgrounds of these people also differ from the early immigrants who were sojourners. The new immigrants are more educated and came originally from urban areas in China. They all lived in Hong Kong, Macao, or in Taiwan for a period of time. Their goal in coming to America is economic betterment. Unlike the sojourners of the past, the new immigrants came here to stay and to make their permanent homes in America. As new immigrants, they had to work very hard, and due to this some of the parents lost contact with their children. As a result, most of the Chinese youth gangs come from the new immigrant families. One should not generalize, however, that the new immigrants were unconcerned with the well-being of their children. Far from wanting to neglect their children, the majority of the new immigrants had the well-being of their children uppermost in mind. Many of the new immigrants who were college educated and had good paying jobs in Hong Kong or elsewhere, migrated to the U.S. for the future education (college) of their children. Since 1953, there have been more than 50,000 new immigrants arriving in Chinatown. The majority of them pay close attention to their children. In fact, the new immigrants, while busy making a living, try to transmit their cultural heritage to their children. As all of them speak some Chinese dialect and have some degree of knowledge of Chinese culture, they want to impart this knowledge to their children. They encourage their youngsters, in addition to attending the regular American school system, to attend the Chinese school in Chinatown on Sundays or in the late afternoons during the weekdays. When the majority of the new immigrants discuss their personal feelings about their identity, most of them indicate that they like certain aspects of American culture and certain aspects of Chinese culture. They like the affluence of American society with high technology, efficiency, freedom, democracy, and material comforts. On the other hand, they prefer the Chinese mode of personal relations, which emphasizes humaneness, courtesy, orderliness, and personalism. In all social interactions with other Chinese in Chinatown, they follow this etiquette. They speak Chinese at home, read Chinese newspapers, and hope to rear their children the Chinese way. However, they aspire to the American dream: a house in the suburbs; one or several cars; children attending college.

The new immigrants have been slighted by the old sojourners or even the American-born Chinese for being the "late comers." Economically, as a group, their command of resources such as property, land, money, and businesses cannot rival the established immigrants or the American-born Chinese. However, successful entrepreneurs have already sprung up among the new immigrants, as many of them have the technical know-how and high educational background. Some have, therefore, a hard competitive edge over the old immigrants in the area of knowledge and training. I have seen millionaires amongst the new immigrants. But the majority of them are trying very hard to achieve an economic status similar to that of the lower and middle class of the larger society. Because of their liking of the Chinese way of life, some of the immigrants prefer to stay in Chinatown. Informant C, who is a new immigrant and has acquired a new residence on Long Island but did not give up his Chinatown apartment, is one of the lucky ones. He told me that:

I like Chinatown for many things. When I first came to New York's Chinatown I was shocked by the dirty and run-down housing and traffic congestion. Now I got a better apartment in the newly established cooperative housing complex in Chinatown; I'd hate to give it up. I take my children to our Long Island residence on weekends. Chinatown has a feeling of warmth to all the Chinese-speaking people. They still address each other as "brother," "sister," "uncle," "aunt," and other traditional respectful names. Of course, you hear Chinese spoken which gives us a sense of intimacy. As for food, you can buy any kind of

Chinese food from Chinatown. You can dine the Chinese way in the restaurants of Chinatown. Many of my friends and relatives work and live here in Chinatown. Moving away from Chinatown will lose many friends. My children can still learn some Chinese from the Chinese language school in Chinatown.

Many new immigrants lament the fact that many American-born Chinese have lost their cultural heritage, and they express the hope that their children will grow up with a dual identity: Chinese and American. As far as China is concerned, the new immigrants have no sympathy for communism, nor do they like Taiwan: They are apolitical in this sense. Many of them suffered under the communist regime while living in China in their early days. Now they have to work very hard, and consequently they lost any interest in participating in political activities. However, they are avid readers of the Chinese newspapers, which keep them informed about international events. A newspaper publisher told me that the new immigrants are the reason for the many Chinese newspapers in Chinatown: There are more than nine Chinese daily newspapers published in New York's Chinatown. Unlike the sojourners of the past, the new immigrants long for naturalization. Those who can speak English want to become citizens as soon as they have accumulated their minimal residency in the U.S., which is five years. As citizens, they can also sponsor their relatives to come to reside in the U.S. Thus, becoming a citizen is also an adaptive decision.

JUMP-SHIP SAILORS AND REFUGEES

The three groups of Chinese in Chinatown, New York have distinctive cultural orientations and have defined their ethnic identity in different ways. There are other subgroups, too: Two of them are the jump-ship sailors and the refugees (boat people from Southeast Asia). The jump-ship sailors and the refugee group are not interested in the question of ethnic identity. They simply have no leisure time to think about it. All they know is that they are of Chinese descent and that they have to work very hard to earn a living to maintain a minimal comfortable way of life. They are concerned with short-term and immediate goals and are willing to work odd jobs and put up with temporary adversities. Both these groups are objects of economic exploitation. They work long hours for less pay. Circumstances and harsh economic reality have made them endure hardship. Many work 18 to 20 hours a day. Slowly and through hard work these two groups of people hope to be able to accumulate enough savings for such things as a stereo, a car, or other modern amenities. For them, there are two major reasons for living in the New World: freedom and material affluence. They also take it for granted that Chinatown is their natural home base for economic activities and for residence. Both groups believe that they are not welcomed by the larger society. As for the jump-ship sailors, their illegal status is an obstacle to working or living outside of Chinatown, New York. The boat people, as they lack the English language skills and knowledge about American society, they prefer to live in a more familiar environment like Chinatown. In fact, since many of them are of Chinese descent and speak the dialect of Chinatown, they requested the U.S. government to relocate them in the Chinatown area. The idea of organizing the Chinese ethnic group into an interest group to participate in the resource distribution in the U.S. society is completely irrelevant to them. Chinatown is simply a convenient place to be because of similarities in linguistic and other cultural practices. Their decisions to work certain jobs, to obtain housing, to marry certain individuals, and to be patient with harsh treatment are guided entirely by practical considerations. They want to establish themselves in America by any means.

THE DISENCHANTED YOUTH

A third subgroup is the disenchanted youth. Chinatown, New York, also has its share of the crime subculture in modern America. Before coming to America, these foreign-born Chinese children or teenagers were brainwashed by American movies, travelers' accounts, and success stories of their American kinsmen or friends, and had unrealistic expectations of the U.S. Some Chinese teenagers, while living in Hong Kong, received remittance from their relatives in America. As the exchange rate between the U.S. dollar and the Hong Kong dollar is five to one, living in Hong Kong on American dollars can be quite comfortable. Some of these teenagers got used to this comfortable living and became disenchanted after their arrival in America, when they soon found out that they had to work long hours and perform only odd jobs in a run-down neighborhood in the Chinatown area. They became quitters and disappointed with the community and with their society. Other children, who transferred from their Chinese schools in Hong Kong to public schools in New York, experienced culture shock, language problems, and academic problems. The "school dropouts" and the quitters from the Chinatown establishments became the favorites of Chinatown's underground, illegal establishments. These groups of young people were the favorite recruits of the illegal gambling dens of Chinatown. They were trained to be "muscle men" and were reimbursed for their criminal activities. Some of these youth gangs went beyond their duties as "muscle men" for the gambling establishments and became racketeers in their own way. They intimidated merchants, practiced extortion, and engaged in gang wars against the rival gangs. Crime became a way of life. They achieved their economic mobility in America through criminal activities they learned in America. From the U.S. environment and from the examples of other criminal gangs, these youth gangs in Chinatown developed their ethnic characteristics. They learned Chinese martial arts, followed some of the practices of the Chinese secret societies in Hong Kong, and thus surrounded themselves with an image of terror. Ethnic chauvenism was strong in these young gangs. They were proud of the Chinese traditional martial arts; in confrontations with other ethnic gangs, the Chinese ethnic gangs wanted to show their "Chinese style of valor." In fact, some Chinese teenagers joined the Chinese gangs only after they had been bullied in schools or in streets by gangs from other ethnic groups, such as the Puerto Ricans and the Blacks. However, the ethnic identity of the Chinese youth gangs was transitory. Their ethnic pride and ethnic chauvenism were intensified only when they were in actual conflicts with other ethnic groups.

All groups of Chinese in Chinatown, regardless of birthplace, identity (or identities) taken, or occupation, have the same aspirations and fears in America. They fear racism in America, especially the repetition of the Japanese–American experience. They are concerned that if things go wrong between PRC-U.S.A. they will become scapegoats. This worry is not entirely unfounded. In the past FBI Chief J. Edgar Hoover indicated that he believed that Chinatown was fifth column for communist China. During the McCarthy era, an American of Chinese descent could easily be accused of being a "communist traitor." In 1954, many Chinese residents and businessmen in Chinatown found themselves objects of scorn: "You Chinese are killing our boys in Korea." It is only after President Nixon's visit to Peking in 1972 that the tide has changed. China is now a friend of the U.S. With movements for social justice, equality, and civil rights for all Americans, Chinese Americans, including citizens and residents, hope that history will not repeat itself and that there will not be the deprivation of civil rights without due process of law just because an individual is of a particular race.

All the Chinese Americans want is to pursue their "American dream"; they want to have enough money to maintain themselves without needing public assistance. They want to achieve economic prosperity through hard work, to be treated equally, and to be free to pursue their careers. They feel that they can make important contributions to American life, but are not given enough recognition by the public. Chinese are still portrayed in the mass media as "Charlie Chan," "Fu Man Chu," "communists," and "illiterates who speak only Pidgin English." It is their wish to see these unfavorable stereotypes erased and to be treated as individuals.

7/Forces of cultural continuity and culture change

New York's Chinatown is an encapsulated urban American community, influenced by both traditional Chinese culture and modern American society. In Chapter 6, the identity crises experienced by various groups of Chinese in Chinatown and the kinds of ethnic identities taken by various subgroups were discussed. The present chapter focuses on the forces of cultural continuity and change in the community. Will Chinese culture survive the Americanization (assimilation) process and become integrated culturally and socially into U.S. society? Will Chinatown resist change and perpetuate its status as an insulated community and as a ghetto or will it follow in the footsteps of some subculture groups and pursue a nativistic movement[1] (i.e., a movement toward reaffirmation of native culture in reaction to the stress of acculturation)? Or will Chinatown change into an interest group based on ethnicity and common destiny? To answer these questions, it is important to identify some of the forces of culture change and continuity.

FORCES OF CULTURAL CONTINUITY

There is no denying that Chinatown is still exotic, retaining many of the traditional Chinese features. There are cultural ties of kinship, language, customs, and values with the Old World. Linguistically, Chinatown uses the dialect commonly spoken in the areas of Canton, Hong Kong, and Macao, although the Sze Yup and Sam Yup dialects are still used by the older immigrants from the rural area of Kwangtung. The families and kinsmen of some of the residents of Chinatown are still in China or Taiwan. And some of the age-old customs (such as belief in certain herbal medicines, practice of the traditional festivals, preference for Chinese food, tendency to associate with people from the same village or locality in China, concern with "face") are still observed in the community, principally by the older immigrants and the new immigrants. The native Chinese-Americans and

[1] For more detail on nativism, see R. Linton, "Nativistic Movements," *American Anthropologist*, 45 (1943), 230–40.

the families of the "stranded intellectuals" have little or no interest in observing many of these traditional customs.

Forces for maintaining the culture emanate from a variety of sources, one of which is the Chinese press. Others include the Chinese School, the traditional associations, and the activities of the *Kiu Ling*. The influx of the new immigrants also serves to reinforce Chinese culture in America. Last, but not least, is the celebration of traditional festivals in Chinatown, some of which are celebrated in public, and others are celebrated privately, either at home or in association halls. Such cultural festivities tend to unite the inhabitants of Chinatown.

The Chinese New Year

By far the biggest and most widely known celebration is the *Chinese New Year* (see Figures 23 and 24). This holiday of the Chinese lunar calendar has been celebrated in all Chinatowns since the 1850s. In New York's Chinatown, street barriers are set up for parades and other festivities. Fireworks, the dragon and lion dances, the colorful banners, and demonstrations of Chinese martial arts can be seen. Groups of lion and dragon dancers representing their respective families, clans, regions, and athletic associations start at the front doors of their association headquarters and proceed to Mott Street, which is the main thoroughfare of Chinatown and where all tourists and residents of the community gather to view

Figure 23   Celebrating the Chinese New Year.

Figure 24   Traditional banners used in the celebration of the Chinese New Year.

the celebration. Special food for the occasion is served in some of the Chinese restaurants. Individually, many old immigrants as well as new immigrant families decorate their homes and shower their children with presents. On the New Year greetings are exchanged in the community: "Gung Hey Fat Choy" (Wishing you to make more money).

Chingming and Chungyung

These two festivals (also known as the "Sweeping of the Grave Festivals,") are dedicated to remembering the dead. Chingming is celebrated in the spring (about April 5), and Chungyung in the fall (about October 4). In New York's Chinatown, the family associations select a day in April and a day in October to remember their friends and relatives from their respective family associations. Typically, a chartered bus takes members of the respective associations to Brooklyn's Evergreen Cemetery to pay respects to the deceased and to clean their tombs. Upon their return to the association halls, members celebrate with a common meal. Some family members may also observe the two festivals on their own, by driving to the cemeteries to pay their respects to their loved ones and to decorate the tombs with flowers.

The Dragon Boat Festival

This festival falls on the fifth day of the fifth month of the Chinese calendar and is known also as the "Double Fifth Festival." In traditional China and present-day Hong Kong, it is a day of boat races. The boats are decorated with mythical dragon heads, and the people rowing the boats move their oars in rhythm with the cymbals and gongs of each boat. The festival commemorates a celebrated poet in China who refused to be corrupt and, in protest, committed suicide by drowning. There are no boat races in New York's Chinatown, but special food called "jung" (glutinous rice filled with beans, pork, lotus seeds, and eggs) is available in the food stores and restaurants for the celebration of this holiday. Some families prepare the food at home. Generally, this festival is popular among the new immigrants and older immigrants.

The Mid-Autumn Festival

Next to the Chinese New Year, the Mid-Autumn festival is most popular and is celebrated by many Chinese families on the fifteenth day of the eighth month of the Chinese calendar. According to the lunar calendar, this day falls during the full moon and thus the festival carries many legends. In celebration, moon cakes— large round cakes made of flour and brown sugar, filled with lotus or bean paste— are eaten. Some moon cakes are also filled with ham and nuts. Other important food items are melons, pomegranates, grapes, apples, and peaches. Not only are these foods seasonal in the summer months, but they are also symbols of fertility and longevity. For most of the Chinese families living in Chinatown, this festival is celebrated privately at home.

Other cultural practices in Chinatown include eating Chinese food with chop-sticks and wearing traditional clothing. Wearing traditional garments is not all that popular because it tends to "single out" an individual in a crowd; thus many Chinese have adopted the American style of dress. Most of the Chinese families in New York prefer to eat Chinese food, however. The grocery stores and Chinese restaurants are always heavily patronized by the Chinese public. There are also Chinese movie theaters which show Chinese movies from Hong Kong and Taiwan. Due to the pressure of hectic work schedules and the activities of the youth gangs in these theaters, many Chinese residents are hesitant to go there.

Some of the traditional Chinese virtues are still observed and valued by the older Chinese, including "hospitality," "consideration," "humaneness," and "face." Obviously, Chinese culture is not moribund in New York's Chinatown; there are many forces perpetuating it.

The Chinese Press

The Chinese press plays an important role in preserving Chinese culture in the community. There are now nine Chinese daily newspapers in New York's China-town, all of which are published in the Chinese language: *World Journal, Sing Tao Jih Pao, The United Journal, Sino Daily Express, China Daily News*, the *China Post, China Voice Daily, The China Tribune*, and the *Peimei News*. Of these, four are pro-KMT (Taiwan), two are sympathetic to the People's Republic of China, two are neutral, and one is directed expressly toward the interests of the Chinese in America. Commenting on the importance of serving Chinese Americans, the publisher of *Sino Daily Express* had this to say:

Almost all the Chinese newspapers in New York's Chinatown are focusing on international news. They also tend to engage in conflicts against each other. There are so many community problems and factions in the community, these newspapers serve to disintegrate the community. I would like to organize a newspaper to unify the Chinese and encourage establishing roots in America. We have so many conflicts. It is high time that someone is doing something to consolidate the Chinese in the community. The second major reason why I started this newspaper is that there is a gap about the news coverage. One group of the press is carrying extensive coverage on news about Taiwan, the other, about PRC, the third group of newspapers has a neutral position. This last group tries to be objective and fair in its editorials. It has news about China and Taiwan. However, so far, there is no newspaper addressing the interests of the Chinese American. My newspaper will serve the interests of the Chinese. The philosophy of my paper is to establish roots in America, to fight for the human rights of the Chinese, to participate in democracy.

From this conversation with the publisher, and from a review of newspapers in Chinatown, I learned that the majority of the Chinese newspapers cover news about the world and about Taiwan or China.

With the exception of one or two dailies, none of the newspapers encourages assimilation and active participation in the social and political life in America. On the contrary, almost all of them preach the "superiority" of Chinese culture, and lament racial prejudices, freedom, excessive individuality, and other so-called vices of American culture. All this should not be interpreted as loyalty or allegiance to China or Taiwan. Curiosity about their mother country is natural. Suffice it to say that the majority of the Chinese press is concerned with promoting Chinese ethnic chauvinism rather than involving the Chinese in the politics of the mother country; it is more a cultural orientation than a political orientation. The publishers of the newspapers are immigrants themselves who do not want to live in China or Taiwan.

As many of the residents in Chinatown are literate only in Chinese, they read only the Chinese newspapers. After 1965, with the influx of new immigrants, the readership of the Chinese newspapers has broadened since many of the immigrants were educated in the Chinese school systems of China, Hong Kong, or Taiwan. The fact that Chinatown, New York can support nine profit-making Chinese newspapers indicates not only the existence of large numbers of readers, but also the potential influence of the Chinese press in Chinatown. Their sermons on the "superiority of Chinese culture" have helped to preserve the Chinese culture. The daily newspapers also carry information on Chinese customs, festivals, and history. Hence the Chinese newspapers serve a dual role: they are agents for maintaining Chinese culture as well as entrepreneurs in the field of mass media.

The Chinese School

The CCBA and the 59 traditional associations have been instrumental in establishing and maintaining the Chinese school that teaches the Chinese language, culture, history, dance, and music. It has a kindergarten, grade school, and a high school, and is run by a staff of 60. The school schedule is specially designed to accommodate the children who study in American public schools. It has an evening section, which begins daily at 4:00 P.M., shortly after children are dismissed from regular public schools, and ends at 7:00 P.M. There are programs on Saturdays and Sundays for children who cannot attend on weekdays. The school has a curriculum for preschool, grade school, junior high, and senior high education. The total enrollment of the school has increased from 200 in 1965 to approximately 3000 in 1980. The graduates from the various programs in 1980 alone totaled 497.

Instruction in the Chinese school is conducted in Chinese, with instructional materials that are donated by the Taiwan government. The school is supported by the various traditional associations in the community and the donations of individuals. Fearing that financial aid from the larger society might cause the loss of community control, the board of trustees and the leaders of CCBA have refused any funding or grants from the U.S. government.

The Chinese school serves as a supplement to the regular public schools. For many Chinese students, coping with school problems and homework from two kinds of school systems is a double burden. The majority of students who attend the Chinese school do so under pressure from their China-born parents. Second-generation, American-born Chinese parents have very little interest in the Chinese school.

The Chinese school is the symbol of Chinese culture in Chinatown. Not only does it enculturate the young through various educational programs and the teaching of Chinese language, music, dance, history, philosophy, classics, and literature, it also provides outlets for those Chinese who want to teach and perpetuate Chinese culture in America, and for those who wish to sit on the board of trustees and be patrons of the community.

Kiu Lings (Leaders of the Traditional Associations)

Kiu lings are first-generation Chinese who are generally well-established economically and are concerned with gaining a name for themselves through activities in the family, dialect, and regional associations and the CCBA. A survey of 60 *kiu lings* from the traditional associations revealed that the majority possess similar social, economic, and demographic characteristics: (1) they are between 50 and 70 years old; (2) they were born in China; (3) they have little formal education; (4) more than two-thirds have spent more than 20 years in the United States; and (5) they are entrepreneurs in Chinese restaurants, laundries, garment factories, groceries, and gift stores. Out of these 60 recognized *kiu lings*, only four have college educations. In addition to their roles as leaders of the community, the *kiu lings* envision themselves to be the patrons of Chinese culture, the *real* Chinese. To show their "Chineseness," they are eager to: (1) participate in the twice-a-year ancestor worship and to direct the celebration of the traditional Chinese festivals; (2) secure membership in many traditional associations; and (3) involve themselves in the affairs of the associations.

The *kiu lings* are also patrons of many other traditional celebrations, such as the Chinese New Year. The colorful banners, the Lion Dance Troupe, and the Chinese firecrackers used for the Chinese New Year are financed chiefly by voluntary contributions from the *kiu lings*. They also are the patrons of many community educational and cultural projects. Thus, the *kiu lings* of the Eng Association have financed the oriental architectural addition to the association's building; the rich *kiu lings* of the On Leong Association were instrumental in the construction of the Chinese-style building at Mott and Canal Streets; and the leaders of the Lun Kong Association donated the expensive Chinese furniture (made of rosewood and marble) in their association.

Not only do the *kiu lings* validate their "Chineseness" and their "prestige" through their active participation in Chinese festivals and their extravagant donations to cultural activities, they also promote traditional values. Many anthropologists who study leadership and patronage systems recognize this practice of choosing values and circulating them among followers. The values selected by the *kiu lings* are traditional: *Lai* (or *Li* in Mandarin), politeness and propriety; *Yi Hei* (or *Yi Chi* in Mandarin), trusting righteousness; *Gam Ching* (*Kan Chin* in Mandarin), sentimental friendship; *Min* (*Mien* in Mandarin), face. These values form the basis of leader-follower or patron-client transactions in the community.

As mentioned earlier, the *kiu lings* are the self-appointed patrons and saviors of Chinese culture. They are interested in having a Chinese school in the community to serve their children as well as the children of their clients. Furthermore, education is highly valued by the Chinese and, as a donor or patron for the community's education program, a *kiu ling* will receive the utmost publicity, which can be used for his gain-seeking activities in other areas. The *kiu lings* support the Chinese school. The most powerful *kiu lings* sit on the executive committee of the board of trustees. The leaders of the family, regional, dialectic, and trade associations are trustees of the Chinese school. They also sponsor scholarships. At the time I conducted my research (1981), the president of the board of trustees was also the president of the Chinese Consolidated Benevolent Association. He said the school had no intention of asking for help from the state or federal government. The *kiu lings* want the school to remain autonomous. Thus, a policy of isolationism is deliberately carried out by the community's leaders to prevent possible intervention by the larger society. This phenomenon is not unique to the Chinese. Social scientists who study U.S. ethnic groups point out that most Jews and Catholics in America have not demanded total equality and perpetuate some social distance because they want to maintain their own communities.

Summary

Internal forces from the community and from individuals bind the Chinese to their culture. Community forces are the Chinese press, the Chinese school, and the leaders of the traditional associations; individual forces are Chinese families. The old immigrant families and the new immigrant families tend to adhere more to the practice of Chinese traditions. One explanation for this is that these people were raised in China and are proud of the ancient Chinese cultural heritage that has lasted more than 5000 years; thus they find it difficult to drop the traditional ways of thinking and behaving, and continue the traditional customs.

FORCES OF CULTURE CHANGE

Living in Chinatown, New York is also living in America. The public schools,[2] the social agencies, the churches, and mass media, all insert the influences of the larger society. In addition to these general forces of acculturation, there are also specific forces that hasten the connection between the community and the larger society, such as: (1) the changing attitudes of the larger society toward ethnic groups, as witnessed in the Civil Rights movement and the Affirmative Action programs; (2) the emergence of China in world politics and the normalization of US–China relations; and (3) the activities of the "culture brokers." These forces have changed conservative Chinatown into a community more open to the larger society.

The Changing Attitudes of the Larger Society

Racial discrimination against ethnic groups in general and Chinese in particular has decreased in the past several decades. Before 1940, New York State

[2] Because the majority of the residents are not educated in the U.S., they do not benefit from the efforts toward assimilation in the public schools.

prohibited Chinese immigrants—residents or citizens alike—from participating and entering more than 26 specific occupations (see Chapter 4). After 1940, Chinese engineers and scientists started to be employed in many states. A significant increase of Chinese in the professions came about after the enactment of federal and state legislation removing racial restrictions. Only in 1956 did the General Electric Company begin to recruit Chinese in New York City. Equitable employment opportunities became more available to the Chinese after the Civil Rights legislation of 1964. Understandably, it is difficult to correct a century of discriminatory employment practices in a short time. In 1976 the Supreme Court ruled that the Chinese immigrants who became permanent residents of the United States should be allowed civil service employment. As discrimination eased, contacts with the larger society increased. The process of acculturation into American society quickened. Some Chinatown residents moved to the suburbs and other areas to find work and to settle. The American-born Chinese-American and the educated China-born Chinese-American found themselves accepted into clubs, churches, and other voluntary associations of the larger society. Some of them entered U.S. politics or joined the Democratic or Republican clubs. Those who live outside Chinatown tend to accept the American middle-class ideals and customs.

Interracial marriage between Chinese and non-Chinese also occurs. According to my informants, 20 percent of the marriages in the 20–30 age group in New York City are interracial (see Figure 25). In many Chinese families living outside of Chinatown, children speak only English. As these children are educated

Figure 25   Interracial dating.

in the public school systems in the suburbs, many of the American-born Chinese socialize only with other American-born Chinese or White Americans and have no opportunity to speak the Chinese language. These children internalize middle-class American values while clinging only marginally to some superficial aspects of Chinese heritage. Families of the second or third generation Chinese-Americans are even more acculturated. There is no longer a preference for sons over daughters. The relationships between children and parents have become more democratic and affectionate. Thus, there are changes in the primary and secondary levels of social interaction among these Chinese-Americans.

The trends of acculturation relate positively to acceptance by the larger society. The more they are accepted, the greater the incentive on the part of the Chinese to acculturate; the more they are accepted into employment by the larger society, the faster they move out of Chinatown. For the acculturated Chinese living in the suburbs, Chinatown has become a "shopping center" and a place for occasional social gatherings such as birthday celebrations, weddings, and other such events. The movement away from Chinatown in the past several decades has usually occurred among American-born Chinese who have completed their college educations and have become professionals employed by American companies. The exodus into the suburbs can be accomplished by any Chinese individual who has the money to buy a house and enough skill in the English language to get along in a non-Chinese area. This option has become a real possibility only in the past 20 years. One of the informants told me that he was denied such an opportunity in the 1930s. Although he was a college graduate from an Ivy League school, he was not permitted to practice his profession and was forced to return to the ethnic niche of Chinatown. Today, more than 70,000 Chinese in New York live outside Chinatown, scattered throughout Queens, Brooklyn, upper Manhattan, New Jersey, and Long Island.

The Emergence of the People's Republic of China and U.S.–China Normalization

The emergence of the People's Republic of China and the subsequent normalization of relations between the U.S. and China have brought many changes in the community. First among these is ethnic pride. The residents of the community may not approve of communist politics in China, but they are proud of the fact that an American President took the initiative to visit China and to normalize the relations between the two countries. With China as a friend of the U.S., many Chinese-Americans feel they will no longer be labeled "enemies" and "fifth columnists" because of their cultural heritage, as they had been for years by government officials and citizens of the U.S. Other changes brought about by the normalization include increased business, and cultural and social exchanges between Chinatown and China. Paradoxically, there is also a significant change in the relationship between the larger society and the Chinese community of New York.

Throughout the years, the People's Republic of China had an unstable policy toward the overseas Chinese: It vacillated between hands-off (leaving them on their own), counting them as citizens of China, and encouraging them to assimilate to the host society. This latter policy, encouraging overseas Chinese to be full-fledged members of the host country, is the latest. In official documents, as well as in Chinese newspapers in China and New York's Chinatown, Chinese-Americans are referred to as "Chinese with American citizenship." As such, a Chinese-American traveling in China is treated as a respectable visitor. Chinese people with American passports get their visas processed sooner and receive better hospitality, rooms, and meals. While living in this country, a Chinese with American citizenship is treated better than a Chinese permanent resident. The former can vote, sponsor relatives from China, and has more job opportunities. Many of the jobs in the federal government have U.S. citizenship as a prerequisite. Thus, both China and the U.S. seem to encourage the Chinese to become naturalized citizens.

One of the direct consequences of the U.S.–China normalization is the official recognition of PRC as the legitimate government of China, as opposed to Taiwan. Many Chinese have come to realize that the U.S. is their *home* country, and feel that: "whether we like it or not, the U.S. is our home and we are going to stay." Many Chinese were born and educated here. They have seen neither China or Taiwan and have no real or psychological connection to either country. Thus, in the post U.S.–China normalization period, the Chinese in the U.S. have become more oriented toward the larger society.

U.S.–China normalization also polarized New York's Chinatown. Some members of the community gravitated to the right, and became loyal supporters of Kuomintang of Taiwan. Others became neutral, and some are sympathetic to the People's Republic of China. The newspapers of Chinatown carry on a continuous dialogue or debate. Some authors are for establishment of a political party, called the "Unification Party," among the overseas Chinese to mediate the current conflicts between Taiwan and China and ultimately unify the people on both sides of the Taiwan Strait. Generally, it is the older immigrants and the China-born intellectuals who are interested in this issue. As for the American-born Chinese and for the majority of Chinatown residents, the discussion of unification reminds them of their true home, which is the United States. Conscious about their identity, many Chinese-Americans—both residents and citizens—decided they should make more of a commitment and contribution to the country in which they make their permanent home, rather than to their country of origin from which they or their ancestors migrated.

The U.S.–China normalization also gave momentum to the Chinese-American movement that began in 1965. Initially, the movement consisted of various disjointed liberal groups in Chinatown, New York to fight racism and to assist members of the community to participate in the resource distribution of the city, state, and federal government. Between 1965 and 1972, these liberal groups attempted to organize the community through the establishment of social agencies and community service organizations. Their activities conflicted with the traditional organizations led by the CCBA. Also, no coordination existed among the liberal groups. After 1972, the liberal groups and the left joined forces to become a political force in Chinatown. National organizations addressing the welfare of Chinese-Americans have been established, such as the Organization of Chinese-Americans (founded in 1973) with headquarters in Washington, DC, and the

National Association of Chinese-Americans (founded in 1977). Both organizations claim they are not interested in the politics of any foreign country, but are primarily concerned with the interests of American citizens and residents of Chinese descent.

One point must be reiterated, and that is the reason why these modern organizations are successful in recruiting members. They are successful because of the change in population composition. Since 1965, many of the new immigrants have better educational backgrounds, and unlike the sojourners in the past, the new immigrants are oriented toward the U.S. They are supportive of the activities that help Chinese immigrants participate in American life. One point is clear: The U.S.–China normalization served as a catalyst to sharpen the sense of identity of Chinese-American citizens and residents. It is a force for change, propelling Chinese-Americans to unite and actively participate in American life.

The "Culture Brokers"

In the past two decades, Chinatown, New York saw increased activity from "culture brokers," who were educated in the U.S. but familiar with both Chinatown and the larger society. They want to bridge the gap between the community and the larger society. Some factors responsible for their existence are the availability of funds through Affirmative Action and the Community Development Program (initiated in 1965). Another factor is the influence of the ethnic movements of the 1960s: The Black and Puerto Rican movements set examples for Chinese-Americans. A third factor was the realization of Chinese-Americans that they are still a minority and are not fully accepted by the larger society. Although blatant discrimination against the Chinese has subsided since 1945, subtle discrimination still lingered. Thus, many Chinese-Americans were motivated to participate in the struggle against racism and the various ethnic movements for equal opportunities.

Since 1965, the community has seen many social agencies and service organizations staffed by "culture brokers" and "middlemen." Within this group of brokers there are several subgroups, distinguished by age, occupation, birthplace, and place of education. They all perform similar services for the community, hold similar views about the Chinese ethnic identity, and have adopted similar strategies for dealing with the larger society.

Many different people act as brokers: full-time or part-time social workers, student volunteers, American-born Chinese, and China-born professionals. These brokers all: (1) have knowledge about the Chinese ethnic group and the United States society; (2) have higher educations; (3) are dissatisfied with *kiu ling* patrons of the community; (4) are relatively young (between 20 and 40 years of age); (5) are middle-class Chinese-Americans; and (6) are second- and third-generation Chinese-Americans living outside of Chinatown.

Perception of Ethnic Identity

Although the *kiu lings* assume three major identities, the brokers assume only one identity—Chinese-American. Every American who has Chinese blood, regardless of his or her language or birthplace, is a Chinese-American. Almost all of these brokers are affiliated with social agencies such as the Chinatown Foundation, the Chinese Community Service Society, the Chinatown Advisory Council, Chinatown Planning Council, and Chinese Development Council. These brokers assist members of the community by adjusting their visa status, helping to obtain social security benefits for the elderly, helping secure funds for day-care centers, finding jobs for the unemployed, mediating disputes, and providing free legal counsel. In other words, they function as middlemen, who help the Chinese participate in the resource distribution of the larger society. In this way the brokers are also change agents, in the sense that they educate the Chinese in how to participate in the larger society and thus purvey the values of the dominant society.

Since participation in the resource distribution of the larger society needs cooperative effort, the brokers feel that a united front among the Chinese is necessary. In addition to the services they perform, they are eager to awaken ethnic consciousness and create an action group with common culture as a base.

Symbols and Validation for the Awakening of Chinese Consciousness

Like the *kiu ling*, culture brokers also realize that continual expression and validation of Chinese culture are necessary for ethnic solidarity. Symbols are used and the memories of the tragic history of the early Chinese in America are recalled. Chinese are encouraged to wear Chinese clothes, especially during parades and demonstrations. Buttons which read "Asian Power," "Chinese Power," and "Yellow Power" are worn during demonstrations. Leaflets are distributed by some social agencies to inform the Chinese public on how to protect their human rights, how to perform their civic duties, and how to file discrimination suits. The brokers' vision of their roles as "educators" are clear. In the words of one official of the Chinatown Planning Council:

> The Chinese immigrants are generally apathetic about politics because they don't know the American political system. They don't know that the American government is supposed to exist for the benefit of the individual. Many of them still hold the view of the traditional Chinese peasant that it is good to stay away from government, to live in a faraway place, to be separated from the influence of government by high mountains. The majority of the Chinese immigrants take for granted that, because they are a minority group, they therefore have to swallow many grievances. They don't know that they have to fight for their rights in this country. This is America!

The brokers realize that they must have a solid following in order to secure more funds and other resources for the community. Thus they proceed in a manner similar to many ethnic politicians—i.e., consciousness-raising.[3] Such an effort is reflected in a mural depicting the plight of the Chinese in America (see Figure 26). On the left of the mural is the infamous massacre of the Wyoming Rock Stream. The four faces in the middle represent the real, not the stereotyped, Chinese in Chinatown. The train symbolizes the contributions of the early Chinese immigrants

[3] Michael Novak, *The Rise of the Unmeltable Ethnics* (New York: Macmillan, 1964).

who helped build the Central Pacific Railroad. On the left of the train is a Chinese seamstress who is on the same level as the Chinese miner and Chinese railroad builder; they all work hard and live frugally. People told me that this mural was painted for the residents of Chinatown, not for the tourists, by young Chinese-Americans affiliated with the Basement Workshop, Inc. They told me they thought the message of their art work was clear: "Chinese should learn from their past experience—unite and fight for survival."

While raising the ethnic consciousness of the Chinese, these brokers at the same time purvey the values of the larger society such as "government exists for the individual," and "equality for all." Thus, the efforts of the brokers aim to prepare the members of the Chinese ethnic group to participate in the larger society.

The brokers' concept of the Chinese community differs from that of the *kiu ling*'s. The *kiu ling* believe the Chinese community should be governed by the "real Chinese." The brokers believe that every Chinese person concerned with community affairs has the right to conduct community service, regardless of ability to speak the Chinese language. *Kiu lings* insist on hierarchical communication channels for all Chinese, the use of different levels of associations. The brokers of social agencies consider associations obsolete vestiges whose structures are good only for the retired and old Chinese. They believe the associations are inadequate to perform any service for the modern Chinese in Chinatown. The brokers are particularly hostile toward the Chinese Consolidated Benevolent Association, which they consider a symbol of the stronghold for *kiu ling* patrons. Most of the social agencies neither discourage nor encourage the Chinese to join

Figure 26   A Chinese mural in Chinatown (1974).

the various associations. However, the hostility between the associations and the social agencies is felt by most of the Chinese. The agencies have frequently attacked the *kiu lings'* ignorance of urban problems and United States politics, as well as their concern for power and prestige. The brokers do not feel the need to follow rules set down by the *kiu ling* for the conduct of daily affairs among the Chinese.

On the other hand, all Chinese are encouraged to use the facilities and services of the social agencies. In fact, several social agencies have made inventories of the various types of services performed by the social service agencies. In these publications, they emphasize the fact that there is no fee, no favor, and no obligation. The public is frequently reminded that no connection or bribery is needed to use these social agencies. In fact, the welfare functions that were once performed by the family and regional associations have now been taken over by the social agencies.

The Chinese are encouraged by the brokers to use the resources of the larger society. They are told that they do not have to depend on the *kiu lings* for employment, financing, or settling disputes. They are aided and encouraged by the new brokers to gradually participate in the activities of the larger society. As a result of the brokers' activities, the bond between the *kiu ling* and the Chinese public has weakened. Again, while the *kiu lings'* efforts have been to insulate the Chinese from the larger society, the social agency brokers are interested in helping the Chinese break away from this isolation. To achieve such an end, some preparations have to be made. Thus, while the *kiu ling* insists on the Chinese School to preserve Chinese culture in America, the brokers wish to establish an English school or center to teach English to adults and new immigrants so that they can be employed in non-Chinese establishments. In almost every major social agency, there is an English program for the Chinese.

Furthermore, while the *kiu lings* refuse to petition for funding from the larger society for the Chinese School, the brokers deliberately attempt to secure funds from the larger society to establish English centers for adults (see Figure 27). Thus, their different emphases reflect the two opposing ideologies of the brokers and *kiu lings*. The *kiu lings* are for the community's autonomy and for the preservation of Chinese culture; the brokers are for the participation of the ethnic group in the larger society.

Dealing with Outsiders

While the *kiu ling* think of themselves as the indispensable link between the Chinese community and Chinese culture, between China (Taiwan) and the United States, the brokers see themselves as the important link between the Chinese ethnic group and the larger society. Their goal is for the Chinese ethnic group to share the resources of the larger society. Their basic strategy is to use Chinese ethnicity to achieve equal opportunity and equal treatment by the larger society. Two devices are used. They emphasize ethnic identity to develop new positions and patterns to organize activities in those sectors formerly not found in the U.S. society; and they form coalitions with other ethnic groups who are seeking similar goals.

Figure 27   An English language center for the adults.

Dealing with the Dominant Society

The traditional *kiu ling* patrons are mainly entrepreneurs in the ethnic niche. Their contact with the larger society is related to their own ethnic niche, as they seek protection of their own economic interests from the larger society. The new brokers, on the other hand, go beyond the activities in these sectors. Knowing that Chinese restaurants, garment factories, laundries, groceries, and gift stores are still the important businesses of the Chinese, the new brokers attempt to render services to people in these areas. For instance, the Chinatown Planning Council has been trying to get federal and city subsidies to run day-care centers for children of Chinese seamstresses who, out of economic necessity, have to work in garment factories and leave young children unattended. They encourage Chinese-Americans to seek employment in all fields, from hospital administration, civil service, construction, and commercial occupations to professional positions. Notices about possible employment with the police and FBI are posted in many social agencies. The agency brokers are interested in placing qualified Chinese in positions in the larger society where they were not formerly found, such as New York Telephone, Con Edison, the U.S. Postal Service, city government, and the broadcasting industry. They also take complaints concerning violations of human rights, Equal Opportunity, and Affirmative Action programs and send them to the proper authorities. Since some of these brokers are volunteers from the legal profession or related fields, they are relatively familiar with procedures for obtaining the attention of the proper authorities.

The community's agency brokers are cognizant of all available resources that the Chinese ethnic group can tap. To compete for these resources, they enlist the aid of American politicians. Politicians who are known to be sympathetic to the Chinese include Bella Abzug (D-New York) and Percy Sutton (Borough President, Manhattan), and they have become household names in the community. Moreover, brokers rouse community support for Chinese candidates who are interested in running for government office in New York. However, because of the limited number of registered voters, it is unlikely that any Chinese candidates will receive the backing of the Chinese community in the near future. However, the need for Chinese politicians is gradually being felt in the community, and the brokers have persuaded many Chinese to register to vote. A few years ago, Chinatown had hardly any Democrats, whereas today there are more than 200 registered Democrats in Chinatown. The number of registered Republicans is much larger.

Some personal histories of the non-*kiu ling* brokers will demonstrate their activities.

Mr. Irving Chin is active in the Community Service Society and the Chinatown Foundation. He is a second-generation Chinese-American from a wealthy restaurant family in Boston. Trained as a lawyer from Yale University Law School, Chin practices his profession in a Wall Street Law firm. He volunteers his services to the Chinese through the aforementioned agencies, and several years ago he was appointed by Mayor Lindsay to the Human Rights Commission. He also helps Chinese fight discrimination in housing and employment.

Father Tong is a clergyman trained at the Yale Divinity School who was recently appointed as the pastor of the Episcopalian Chapel in Chinatown. He openly supports the Chinese-American movement and the radical youth groups and thus irritates many of the *kiu lings*. He is also a member of the board of directors of the Chinatown Planning Council and is instrumental in many of its decision-making activities. Some years ago he proposed to the diocese a plan to build a multiservice center for Chinatown to provide space and financial aid for all social agencies. In response to his suggestion, his diocese bought two buildings, one with a gymnasium for the reactional activities of the teenagers.

Professor X is a foreign-born Chinese-American, who received his professional training in the United States. Together with some other Chinese university professors in the metropolitan area, he formed an organization called the National American-Chinese Civic Association, whose purpose is to mobilize community residents for social action. Since he and his colleagues were born in China but educated in the U.S., he thinks they are in a position to unite all the various factions, such as the traditional CCBA and the Chinese-American movement, in a common cause. The ultimate hope of Professor X is that as a minority group the Chinese may enjoy a stronger bargaining power in American society.

Not all the people who come to Chinatown to perform brokerage functions do so for ideological purposes. Some establish agencies because resources have been allocated for community service by the Office of Economic Opportunity, and full-time social workers who perform brokerage functions in the federal or state funded social agencies receive competitive salaries. Other brokers come to help the Chinese because of political ambitions: They hope to gain votes for future campaigns.

The number of Chinese-American college students who return to Chinatown to help community development has been on the increase. These students are particularly zealous in assisting the Chinese in fighting for equal treatment and equal opportunity from the dominant society. Basically, these brokers use the conflict approach—not conflict in the sense of physical force but in the sense of social pressure and mental attitudes. The brokers feel that the American way is to fight for equality and freedom, and they are fond of using methods commonly resorted to by many interest groups in America, such as protests, demonstrations, and strikes. They also want to form coalitions with other ethnic groups to protest and fight for equal rights and create new social positions. This approach contrasts sharply with that of the *kiu lings*, who insist on harmony, patience, and inaction unless necessary. Having experienced prejudice and discrimination in their early years, many of the *kiu lings* simply think that publicity and visibility will only create unhappy consequences and bring disaster to the community. The *kiu ling* normally think the measures of the brokers are too drastic and do not approve of such actions.

Coalitions with Other Ethnic Groups

Fredrik Barth (1969) pointed out that the strategy of using ethnic identity to create new social positions and organize activities not formerly found in the larger society could generate sound movements such as nativistic and separatist movements, as well as new political alliances.[4] The emergence of the Chinese-American movement and the alliance of the Chinese with the Japanese and other Asians are cases in point. All these movements have been organized on the basis of ethnicity. The Chinese-American movement uses the Chinese identity; the Asian American movement uses a larger ethnic identity (Asia). The manipulation of regional ethnicity for goal-seeking activities is also recognized by Lyman and Douglas (1973: 344–365).[5] Certain situations dictate an appropriate ethnic choice and an individual has to respond by assuming an appropriate ethnic identity:

> Thus, the American-born son of immigrant parents from Canton might find it advantageous to invoke his membership in the Sam Yup speech group when interacting with a speaker of Sze Yup dialect; in the Cantonese regional group when encountering a fellow from Shanghai; in the Chinese "race," when confronting whites; in the Asian people, when forming an ethnic studies program; and as an oriental, when discussing the influence of cultures on behavior. Moreover, he may find it to be fun or profitable to be "Japanese" when seeking a date with a nisei girl; to be "Hawaiian" when confronting people interested in peoples from exotic and tropical environments; and to be "just plain American" when seeking a job.[6]

Although the *kiu lings* assume several subethnic identities, such as the real Chinese, the overseas Chinese, the American Chinese, or even Cantonese-Chinese or Toysanese-Chinese, they never feel comfortable assuming the Asian identity.

[4] This is a seminal work on ethnicity. For more detail, see Fredrik Barth, *Ethnic Groups and Boundaries* (Oslo: Universitetes for Laget, 1964).
[5] Lyman Stanford and William Douglas, "Ethnicity: Strategies of Collective and Individual Impression Management," *Social Research*, 40:2 (1973), 345–365.
[6] Ibid., p. 355.

This is partly because they prefer to keep their distance from other ethnic groups and maintain the autonomy of the Chinese ethnic group. In the case of the organizers of the Chinese-American movement, they understand that if they want to make an impact on the larger society, they need more participants. Thus, it is advantageous to incorporate with other Asian peoples to form a movement to fight racism.

It is not just the need for more members that has caused Chinese-Americans to cooperate with other Asians. Common interests and destiny are also important bases for the coalition. Japanese, Chinese, Koreans, and other Asians are frequently referred to in official legislation and documents as Asians or Orientals. If one Asian group, say the Japanese, breaks a racist barrier, it is likely that the Chinese and other Asians will also benefit. So far, all Asian groups have cooperated in their struggle for equal opportunity and human rights.

The Chinese-American movement was organized in Chinatown in 1970 by a group of rather militant United States-born, college-age, Chinese-Americans, who intended to awaken the ethnic consciousness and ethnic power of the Chinese by publishing a bilingual newspaper, *Getting Together*. They also organized antiwar and antitourist demonstrations in Chinatown. However, very few Chinatown residents were enthusiastic about the movement, and even fewer participated in the demonstrations. The *kiu lings* were particularly hostile to the organizers of the Chinese-American movement because they thought the members of the movement were basically pro-Communist radicals who opposed the power structure of the CCBA, and thus their activities were bad for tourist business in Chinatown. Because of the emergence of ethnic consciousness, the Chinese-American movement has recently gained more members. They have also affiliated with established agencies such as the Youth Mobilization and the Chinatown Planning Council to render their free "brokerage" services to the Chinese and help them to participate in the resource distribution of the larger society.

These brokers are middle-class Chinese-Americans, many of whom do not live in Chinatown. Some live in the affluent suburbs or neighborhoods of New York City, yet they retain their ethnic identity. Moving to an "American" neighborhood does not necessarily wipe out ethnic identity. Most social scientists agree that it is possible for members of an ethnic group to take up the American way of speaking, dressing, and living and at the same time retain their ethnicity.

Some of the reasons that ethnic groups have survived in America are: (1) early childhood socialization processes have passed on to children many unconsciously ethnic traits and behavioral patterns; (2) ethnic groups are sometimes deliberately maintained and used to carry on cultural tradition; (3) ethnic groups are advantageous and are used as interest groups for social, political, and economic activities; (4) ethnic self-identification is a component of personal identity for many members of ethnic groups; and (5) people are more comfortable interacting with other people whose feelings, values, instincts, and beliefs are similar to their own.

In summary, the new brokers from the social agencies and youth organizations follow a strategy directly opposed to that of the *kiu lings*. They use ethnicity to participate in the social, economic, and political life of the larger society. The *kiu lings*, on the other hand, want to isolate the community from the larger society and maintain a closed community in which the *kiu lings* serve as patrons who control the community and preserve the status quo. As a consequence of the new brokers' activities, the Chinese community of New York has become more outward oriented, and the ethnic boundary of the community has assumed a different character from that of pre-1965 Chinatown. Formerly, the Chinese ethnic boundary was almost impenetrable. Today, New York's Chinese community does not disclaim social, economic, or welfare assistance from the larger society, nor does it isolate the members of the community from participation in the social, economic, and political resources of the larger society.

8/Conclusion: the future of Chinatown

Chinatown, New York is neither Chinese nor American. Rather, it represents the Chinese adaptation to American life. It reflects American racism, social and economic adaptation of an ethnic group, and the dilemma of ethnic identity in modern American life. This case study has demonstrated the social organization, economic activities, family life, and ethnic identities of the Chinese and how their way of life was the result of adaptation to the American environment. Culture, as well as cultural institutions change, and as changes take place in the larger system, the encapsulated subcultural system is affected. In the past several decades, both China and the U.S. have experienced rapid changes socially, politically, and diplomatically. Chinatown, New York is also caught in the turmoil of the social and political change of the larger system. Organizationally, the CCBA-led traditionalist organizations that were patterned after Chinese kinship, regional, linguistic similarities, and hometown affinities are still active. As a whole, they are conservative, pro-Kuomintang, anti-assimilation. In their effort to maintain the community's autonomy and to protect the interests of the power elite and the traditional entrepreneurs, the traditional social structure has insulated the community from the larger society. The modernist organizations led by Chinatown Planning Council and other social agencies have steadily gained footage in the community. The U.S.-oriented organizations have helped the members of the community to obtain their goals by using methods of the larger society: politicization, confrontation tactics (petitions, demonstrations, strikes), organizing the community into an interest group.

The community has become more heterogeneous in the post-1965 era. Population has increased and the physical boundary has been expanded. The growth of Chinatown is accompanied by many growing pains: problems with youth gangs, problems of housing, medicare, aging, childcare, labor disputes, social inequality. Some of these problems themselves are subjects of social workers' studies and, as they are beyond the scope of this study, they have not been discussed in detail. Suffice it to say that these practical topics can be reviewed by students of ethnicity, sociology, anthropology, as well as social work as problems for term papers and field research projects.

Although the community is experiencing rapid change, there is no indication that Chinatown, New York is disintegrating under the pressures of acculturation from New York City. It is an older community with more than 130 years of history and with a population of 70,000. While many of the urban ethnic groups have completely integrated into the larger society, there are reasons (as discussed in Chapters 6 and 7) to believe that Chinatown, New York will exist for a long time. What will be changed is the nature of Chinese ethnicity. The process of change has already started, transforming Chinatown from an urban ethnic ghetto into an interest group based on a common culture. This is the process of Americanization. Chinatown is adapting to the changing American environment.

Bibliography

Barth, Fredrik (ed.), 1969, *Ethnic Groups and Boundaries*. Oslo: Universitetes for Laget.

Barth, Gunther Paul, 1964, *Bitter Strength: A History of the Chinese in the United States, 1850–1870*. Cambridge, Mass.: Harvard University Press.

Beck, L., 1898, *New York's Chinatown*. New York: Bohemia Publishing Co.

Berger, Mike, 1957, "New York Chinatown," *Fiftieth Anniversary*. New York: Chinese Chamber of Commerce.

Cattell, Stuart, 1970, *Health, Welfare and Social Organization in Chinatown*. New York City: Community Service Society (mimeograph).

Chen, Ta, 1923, *Chinese Migration with Special Reference to Labour Conditions*. United States Bureau of Labor Statistics, No. 340.

———, 1940, *Emigrant Communities in South China*. New York: Institute of Pacific Relations.

Cheng, David Te-Cha'o, 1948, *Acculturation of the Chinese in the U.S.: A Philadelphia Study*. Foochow, China.

Chinatown Health Project, 1970, *Chinatown Health Project Report* (manuscript). New York.

Chinatown Study Group, 1969, *Chinatown Study Group Report* (manuscript). New York.

Chu, Y. K., 1975, *History of the Chinese People in America*. New York: The China Times (in Chinese).

Consolidated Chinese Benevolent Association, 1948, *By-Laws of the Consolidated Chinese Benevolent Association*, rev. ed. New York: CCBA.

Coolidge, Mary Roberts, 1969, *Chinese Immigration*. New York: Arno Press.

Fried, Morton, 1958, *Colloquium on Overseas Chinese*. New York: Institute of Pacific Relations.

Glazer, Nathan, and Daniel Moynihan, 1963, *Beyond the Melting Pot*. Cambridge, Mass.: MIT Press.

Gordon, Milton M., 1964, *Assimilation in American Life*. New York: Oxford University Press.

Greeley, Andrew M., 1971, *Why Can't They Be Like Us?* New York: E.P. Dutton.

Hoy, William, 1942, *The Chinese Six Companies*. San Francisco: California Chinese Historical Society.

Hsu, Francis L.K., 1971, *The Challenge of the American Dream*. Belmont: Wadsworth.

Kramer, Judith R., 1971, *The American Minority Community*. New York: Thomas Y. Crowell.

Kung, S.W., 1962, *Chinese in American Life: Some Aspects of Their History, Status, Problems and Contributions*. Seattle: University of Washington Press.

Kuo, Chia-ling, 1977, *Social and Political Change in New York's Chinatown*. New York: Praeger.

Lang, Olga, 1946, *The Chinese Family and Society*. New Haven: Yale University Press.

Lee, James, 1972, "The Story of the New York Chinese Consolidated Benevolent Association." *Bridge Magazine*, 1(3):15–18.

Lee, Rose Hum, 1960, *The Chinese in the United States of America*. Hong Kong: Hong Kong University Press.

Lyman, Stanford, and William Douglas, 1973, "Ethnicity: Strategies of Collective and Individual Impression Management." *Social Research*, 40(92):345–365.

Miller, Stuart Creighton, 1969, *The Unwelcome Immigrant*. Berkeley and Los Angeles: University of California Press.

Morse, Hosea, 1918, *The International Relations of the Chinese Empire*. London: Longmans Green.

Novak, Michael, 1972, *The Rise of the Unmeltable Ethnics*. New York: Macmillan.

Paine, Robert (ed.), 1971, *Patrons and Brokers in the East Arctic*. Newfoundland: Institute of Social and Economic Research, Memorial University of Newfoundland.

Sung, Betty Lee, 1967, *Mountain of Gold*. New York: Macmillan.

———, 1976, *A Survey of Chinese-American Manpower and Employment*. New York: Praeger.

Wong, Bernard, 1976, "Social Stratification, Adaptive Strategies and the Chinese Community of New York." *Urban Life*, 5(1):33–52.

———, 1977, "Elites and Ethnic Boundary Maintenance: A Study of the Roles of Elites in Chinatown, New York City." *Urban Anthropology*, 6(1):1–25. Also in *Urban Place and Process*, Press and Smith (eds.). New York: Macmillan, 1980, pp. 402–421.

———, 1978, "A Comparative Study of the Assimilation of the Chinese in New York City and Lima, Peru." *Comparative Studies in Society and History*, 20(3):335–358.

———, 1979, *A Chinese American Community*. Singapore: Chopmen Enterprises.

Wu, Chang-tsu, 1958, "Chinese People and Chinatown in New York City." Ph.D. Thesis. Ann Arbor: University Microfilms.

———, 1972, *"Chink!" A Documentary History of Anti-Chinese Prejudice in America*. New York: World Publications.

Yuan, D.Y., 1963, "Voluntary Segregation: A Study of New York's Chinatown." *Phylon*, 24(3):255–268.

———, 1966, "Chinatown and Beyond: The Chinese Population in Metropolitan New York." *Phylon*, 27(4):321–332.